W9-BKU-809
WITHDRAWN

Great Americana

Route across the Rocky Mountains

Overton Johnson and William H. Winter

Route across the Rocky Mountains

by Overton Johnson
and William H. Winter

READEX MICROPRINT

LIBRARY OF CONGRESS CATALOG CARD NO. 66-26352

MANUFACTURED IN THE UNITED STATES OF AMERICA

Foreword

In the 1840's in the farmhouses of Missouri, Indiana, Illinois, and Iowa excitement about a new frontier in the Far West was causing much talk. Soon "Oregon fever" was running high and emigrants were discussing the best way of getting to the new promised land on the Pacific coast. News of the fertile valleys of the Willamette and the lower Columbia had spread rapidly as the result of letters sent back by missionaries. By 1843, a great wave of emigration had set in, and wagon trains of emigrants were stretched out along the "Oregon Trail" all the way from Independence, Missouri (the usual point of departure), to the Columbia River. Two of the participants in the great migration of 1843 were Overton Johnson and William H. Winter, who wrote a narrative of their journey and a description of the country for the benefit of future travellers. Their book, *Route Across the Rocky Mountains, with a Description of Oregon and California,* was published in Lafayette, Indiana, in 1846. A modern edition with explanatory preface and notes by Carl L. Cannon was brought out in 1932 by the Princeton University Press.

The Oregon country was first exploited by the fur traders. The American Fur Company established a base, Astoria, at the mouth of the Columbia River in 1811. In 1813 Astor's company sold the little post to the Northwest Company, which became a part of the Hudson's Bay Company in 1821, with Dr. John McLoughlin as virtual ruler in Oregon. McLoughlin welcomed American Methodist missionaries led by the Reverend Jason Lee, who first came to Oregon in 1832. In 1836, Presbyterians, led by Dr. Marcus Whitman, established a mission in the Walla Walla Indian country, at the junction of the Columbia and Snake rivers.

The missionaries sent back glowing reports of the fertility of the soil, the salubriousness of the climate, the abundance of game and fish, and, in short, the almost celestial attractions of the country. Missionary letters were published in weekly papers in the Midwest and in other parts of the country. In addition, Washington Irving had made literary capital out of the trip made by Captain Benjamin Bonneville, who took the first wagon train across South Pass and down the Snake and Columbia rivers. Irving's *Astoria* (1836) and his *Adventures of Captain Bonneville, U.S.A.* (1837) whipped up fresh interest in the Northwest.

The Oregon country was still in dispute between Great Britain and the United States when American settlers began to pour into the country. In 1818 an agreement had been reached between the two countries for joint occupancy until the boundary could be established, but it was not until June 15, 1846, that the dispute was finally settled.

Overton and Winter's *Route Across the Rocky Mountains* is valuable because it is a realistic narrative that discounts some of the more romantic notions of the country put in circulation by Irving and the missionary letters. "Many of the accounts given of those countries [the Northwest] are too flattering," the authors point out; "and again, on the contrary, some make their disadvantages to appear greater than they really are.... The world contains now no Garden of Eden. There is no particular portion of the habitable globe that possesses advantages greatly superior to the rest. If one has a better climate, the other has a better soil; if one has a better commercial situation, the other has some counter-balancing advantage sufficient to make them nearly or quite equal." An account of their "long and tedious tour," the authors think, will be of use to the public, and for that reason they have prepared it for the press.

The narrative is detailed and often entertaining. The authors have little good to report of the Indians, and they dislike English sportsmen, like Sir William Stewart, who come on hunting expeditions to the West, scatter the buffalo, and make it difficult for parties in need of food to kill game. Their information is not invariably accurate but is always interesting. Santa Barbara they place twenty miles from the coast. Their spelling and diction are sometimes original. San Joaquin, for example, they spell phonetically, St. Wakine. The narrative concludes with a useful appendix, "Instructions to Emigrants—Supplies and Equipment—Manner of Travelling, &c.—Bill of the Route." This last gives mileages between points from Independence to the mouth of the Columbia. In addition to the information in the annotated version of the narrative, published by the Princeton University Press, background material about Oregon in this period will be found in Ray Billington, *Westward Expansion* (New York, 1949).

ROUTE

ACROSS THE ROCKY MOUNTAINS,

WITH A

DESCRIPTION OF OREGON AND CALIFORNIA;

THEIR

GEOGRAPHICAL FEATURES, THEIR RESOURCES, SOIL, CLIMATE, PRODUCTIONS, &c., &c.

BY OVERTON JOHNSON AND WM. H. WINTER,
OF THE EMIGRATION OF 1843.

LAFAYETTE, IND:
JOHN B. SEMANS, PRINTER.
1846.

PREFACE.

FROM the general interest manifested by the People of the United States, and particularly that portion residing in the great Valley of the Mississippi, in regard to the Territory of Oregon and the Province of California, we have been impressed with the belief, that any correct information concerning those countries, clad in ever so homely and unpretending a garb, would be received by them with favor. From this conviction, and indulging the hope that a long and tedious tour, might thus be turned to public as well as individual advantage, we have concluded to give the following pages to the press.

There is, we suppose, no portion of North America, East of that great dividing chain—the Rocky Mountains—similar to that on the West. The general features of the country, the climate, the soil, vegetation, all are different. Nature appears to have created there, upon a grander scale. The mountains are vast; the rivers are majestic; the vegetation is of a giant kind; the climate, in the same latitude, is much milder. The soil, generally, is inferior to that of the Western States. Many of the valleys, in point of fertility, are, perhaps, unsurpassed; but to compare the whole country with an equal portion of the Western States, it is much inferior.

Only a small portion of those territories laid down on the maps as Oregon and California, are at all calculated for settlement: much the largest portion of both, are nothing more than barren wastes, which can yield little or nothing to the support of animal life. The valuable portion of Oregon lies between the Blue Mountains and the Coast; and the valuable portion of California, between the California Mountains and the Coast. The principal advantages that those countries possess over the Western States, are a mild and very healthy climate, and an excellent commercial situation.

Our description of those countries, we are aware, will differ, in many respects, from those which have been, and that probably will be given, by others; for, as men are constituted differently, with different faculties, with different tastes and inclinations; so they differ in their opinions in regard to things. It is impossible for all to view the same things with the same eye. The same situation, the same soil, the same climate, the same country, is not—cannot be, adapted to the wishes and wants of all; therefore, though the thing described be the same, there will be a slight difference of coloring in the descriptions of different persons, which will to some extent convey different ideas to the mind of the same reader. Many of the accounts given of those countries are too flattering; and, again, on the contrary, some make their disadvantages to appear greater than they really are. These different descriptions have not always been given to mislead; but are frequently the offspring of the differing judgment of those who have written. Some will probably form opinions from our statements, and some may be induced to visit or emigrate to those distant Western shores; and if such should be the case, they may be disappointed in their expectations, and find countries differing widely from the pictures they had drawn. It is difficult to form a correct idea of a country from any description that can be given. Men are apt to expect too much—to draw their pictures too fair; they look to those wild and distant regions for something surpassing nature, and they are disappointed. The world contains now no Garden of Eden. There is no particular portion of the habitable globe that possesses advantages greatly superior to the rest. If one has a better climate, the other has a better soil; if one has a better commercial situation, the other has some counterbalancing advantage, sufficient to make them nearly or quite equal.

The route to California, the description of that country, and the return from it to Fort Hall, are from the notes of Wm. H. Winter.

CONTENTS.

CHAPTER I.

CHAPTER II.

CHAPTER III.

CHAPTER IV.

CHAPTER V.

CHAPTER VI.

CHAPTER VII.

CHAPTER VIII.

JOURNAL.

CHAPTER I.

THE JOURNEY OUT, WITH ITS INCIDENTS.

Departure from Independence—Country of the Shawnee and Kanzas Indians—Rainy Weather and muddy traveling—Antelopes and Prairie Dogs—Cold Rain Storm on the Platte—Buffalo region—Sand Hills—Pawnee and Sioux Indians—Forts on the Platte—Black Hills—Red Butes—Killing a Grizley Bear—Sulphur Springs—Summit of the Rocky Mountains.

In the latter part of May, 1843, we left Independence. a small town in the Western part of the State of Missouri, situated six miles South of the Missouri River and twelve miles from the Western line of the State, and now the principal starting point for all the companies engaged in the Western and New Mexican trade, and place of general rendezvous of persons from all parts of the United States, wishing to emgirate or travel beyond the Rocky Mountains. In a few hours we passed the Western boundary of the State, and came into the territory of the Shawnee Indians. They occupy a small, but very beautiful and fertile country, laying immediately West of the State line. The Shawnees have made considerable advancement towards civilization. Many of them have good farms and comfortable houses. Some of them are good Mechanics, and most of them speak the English language tolerably well.

We were traveling here in the great Santa Fé trace, and again and again, we passed long trains of Merchant wagons, laden with the products of our Manufactories and other Merchandize, and bearing them afar across the deserts, to be exchanged for the gold and silver of the Provinces of Mexico. This trace is large, and as well beaten, as many of the most important public highways in the States.

After leaving the country of the Shawnees, we came next into that of the Kanzas Indians. Their's, also, is a very beautiful country; entirely in a state of nature. It differs but little from the Western part of Missouri, except that the surface is more undulating, and that it has less timber. Here we left the last traces of civilization, and seemed, for a time, to be beyond even the borders of animated existence. Not even the song of a bird broke upon the surrounding stillness; and, save the single track of the Emigrants, winding away over the hills, not a foot print broke the rich, unvaried verdure of the broad forest-begirt prairies; and in the little islet groves that dotted the plain—the wooded strips that wound along with the course of the rivulet—and the blue wall that surrounded, not a trunk was scarred nor a twig was broken. It was a vast, beautiful and perfect picture, which nature herself had drawn, and the hand of man had never violated. No decoration of art, mingled to confuse or mar the perfection. All was natural, beautiful, unbroken. The transition had been sudden, as the change was great. Every thing was calculated to inspire the mind with feelings of no common kind. He alone, who for the first time stands upon the deck of some tall ship, whose sails are spread before the breeze, and whose foaming prow looks steadily towards some distant clime, when for the first time he sees the loved shores of his native land sink into the wave, and the blue waters of the treacherous deep gather around him, may appreciate the sensations which awakened in our hearts, when here we reflected upon where we were, and what we had undertaken: when the past; all that we had left behind us—nothing less than the whole civilized world, with all of its luxuries, comforts, and most of its real necessities—society, friends, home,—all that is in this world dear to man:—when the future, dark and uncertain—presenting nothing but a vast extent of drear and desert wastes, uninhabited save by the wild beast and savage—filled, perhaps, with thousands of unknown difficulties and dangers, hardships and privations,—rushed at once, in mingled confusion, upon the mind, and impressed upon our feelings a full sense of the loneliness of our situation and the rapidly increasing space that was separating us from from all communion with the civilized world.

The morning had been fair, and we were moving slowly along

through the middle of one of the wide prairies, without noticing the cloud which had been gathering in the North, until its thunders awoke us from our dreaming. The breeze, which before had scarcely stirred the grass upon the plain, grown into a gale, now roared over the hills. The rain soon followed, pouring in torrents. Our mules, wheeling with their heads from the storm, refused to proceed. We were therefore compelled quietly to endure it, and wait upon the pleasure of our long eared masters. Fortunately, it lasted for but little more than an hour; but this was sufficient for us to become completely drenched with the rain and chilled with the cold. But in a short time the cloud passed over, and the rays of the sun having dried our garments and tempered the atmosphere to its previous mildness, made every thing appear more cheerful than before.

This we regarded as a sort of introduction to the next six months. As the sun approached the horizon, we turned aside and halted, on the bank of a small creek, and made preparations to pass the night. We turned our animals loose to graze, having first fastened strong cords, about ten yards in length, about their necks, that we might not have difficulty in catching them. After they had run loose some time, one end of the cord was fastened to a stake, to prevent their rambling away, through the night, and the rope was sufficiently long to give them room to feed plentifully. Having pitched our tent and kindled a fire, supper was soon prepared, spread upon the ground, and we took our seats upon the grass around it. Three articles—bread, meat and coffee—completed the variety of the board; and although they were not prepared in the neatest and most tasteful manner, yet our appetites spoke abundant praises for the ability of the cook. Supper being finished, as the night grew dark, we retired one by one to rest, spreading our beds upon the ground. We slept to dream of all that we loved and had left behind us, and awoke to know that they were far from us and that our home was the wild uncultivated field of nature, "whose walls the hills and forests were, whose canopy the sky." Having traveled up the Kanzas River 90 miles, we came, on the 30th of May, to where the Emigrants were crossing. We saw here the first village of Kanzas Indians. Their huts are made of poles and bark, and are about sixteen feet wide, by thirty long, and eight high. The ends are perpendicular, but the sides joining with the roof in a gradual curve, make the whole very nearly in the shape of the half of a circular cylinder. They were very filthy and almost entirely naked, not disposed to be hostile to the whites, but like most other Indians, they are expert and inveterate thevies. The River not being fordable, the Emigrants constructed two large canoes, which they fastened together at a sufficient distance apart, by a platform of round poles laid across and extending from one end to the other. Upon this they placed the wagons by hand, and ferried them across the stream. The cattle and horses were turned loose and made to swim to the opposite shore. We succeeded in getting across on the same day that we arrived, and after delaying one day and a half, endeavoring to make up a small company to precede the main body and follow on the trail of Mr. Wm. Sublet and Sir Wm. Stewart, who were ahead, with a company of men, on a party of pleasure to the Mountains, we succeeded in making our company eight persons, and again began to travel.

The Emigrants, amounting, in all, to about six hundred persons, after they had finished crossing, organized themselves into a sort of traveling Government; adopted a short code of laws, employed a pilot, and elected a captain and officers of the guard. We still continued to travel up the Kanzas; but leaving it further and further to the left. The valley of this stream is high rolling prairies, and is very fertile. Its bottoms are wide, and there are numerous br[illegible]nches coming in from both sides, on all of which there is timber [illegible] ost varieties found West of the Mississippi, some of which is

[illegible]

[illegible]nety miles above our crossing, we came to and crossed Big Bl[illegible] River, one of its main branches. Here the Emigrants came up with us, and it was late in the night before their last wagons got over. This region has the character of being the residence of storms, and immediately after our arrival some of the blustering inhabitants introduced themselves in a manner that was by no means agreeable. After the sun went down, a dense black cloud covered the sky, from which the rain fell in torrents during the whole night. The extreme darkness was dispelled by the dazzling and incessant flashes of lightning. The thunder kept up a constant roar, and frequently its sharp peals resembled the discharge of volleys of artillery. The wind blew so high that most of the tents were thrown down, and one of the wagons was fairly blown over. The surface of the ground was flooded with water, and in the morning we found the River, which we had crossed on the past evening without difficulty, had risen so rapidly as to overflow its bottoms near one fourth of a mile on either side, and was entirely impassable.

This is the middle ground between the Kanzas and Pawnee Indians. The day before we crossed the Big Blue River, we met a war party of Kaus, (Kanzas,) returning from the Pawnee country. They told us they had seen the Pawnees, and had beaten them in battle; but we learned afterwards, from a more creditable source, that it was exactly the other way. They had one or two fresh scalps and as many wounded men, and were leaving the world behind them as fast as possible. We saw their battle-ground afterwards, and found on it two or three dead bodies. Here, the Emigrants, finding that it was inconvenient and retarding to their progress, to to travel in so large a body, dissolved their first organization and formed thmselves into smaller companies.

It continued to rain, at intervals, for several days, and the road which had before been as good as we could wish, became quite muddy and bad. After leaving Big Blue River, we continued to travel through a country very similar to that previously described, excepting that the proportion of timber was less, until we came to the Little Blue River—a distance of 70 miles; and here, the hills bordering on the stream, are a little sandy. After striking this stream, we continued to travel up it 50 miles; then leaving it, turned across in a North Westerly direction, for the main Platte River. On the Little Blue River we found a few Antelopes, which were the first wild animals of any size, which we had seen since we left the States; and after leaving the waters of the Kanzas, we found no bees, and this, from all that we could learn, is the farthest point West which they have yet reached: Nor did we find any of the wild fowls, or smaller animals, common in the Western States, until we passed the Mountains. We reached the Platte River in the evening; the distance across being about 25 miles, which is the greatest, on the whole route, without water.

After leaving the waters of the Kanzas, the character of the country changes rapidly. The hills, on either side of the narrow valley of the Platte, which is from five to ten miles wide, are little else than huge piles of sand. The valley itself, is quite sandy; but it nevertheless produces a rich grass, which our animals were very fond of. It is also covered, in many places, with the Prickly Pear, the thorns of which frequently get into the feet of the loose cattle and produce lameness. The River is from one to three miles in width, and the bed of the channel is entirely of quicksand. When we came to it, it was quite full, and the water was every where running level with its banks, but seldom overflow.

ing them, and was running with a strong, even current. There is, in many places along the Platte, a kind of salt, with which the ground, in spots, is covered; and the water in the River is slightly impregnated. In some of the sloughs and pools, back from the River, the water is very strong. We found but little wood here, and none except immediately on the River. We were frequently unable to procure it, and were compelled, sometimes, to make a strange substitute in the excrement of the Buffalo, in order to do our cooking. The varieties of timber are few; the principal kind being what is commonly called Cotton Wood. We saw great numbers of Antelopes, as we passed up the River; but they were so wild, and the valley was so level, that it was difficult to approach them. We also saw a singular little animal, which has been called the Prairie Dog. Its size, shape and color, are very much the same as the large wharf rat, and its barking resembles that of the common Gray Squirrel. They burrow in the ground, and live in villages, frequently of several hundreds. There is a small Owl, that sometimes lives in the same hole with the Dog.

As we were now coming into the game country, and expecting every day to see the plains covered with herds of Buffalo; we made up a hunting party, (having previously joined one of the emigrating parties,) of 20 men, and proceeded up the River ahead of the wagons, to obtain meat and dry it by the time they would come up, in order to make as little detention as possible. In the evening of the second day, we heard the guns of some of the party, who were in chase of a Buffalo along the Southern side of the valley, and as we saw the clouds begin to swell, dark and angrily above the Western horizon, and heard their thunders muttering heavily behind the hills, we thought it prudent to halt and prepare our camp. As we saw no timber ahead, and did not wish to go back, we stopped upon the open prairie, on the nearest high ground to the River. The rain had begun to fall; but several of us, who were anxious to see the Buffalo, disregarding it, mounted our horses and galloped across the valley, in the direction from which we had heard the reports of the guns. The wind was blowing a gale; the clouds grew darker, until they almost shut out the light of the setting sun. The rain increased, and by the time we had reached the spot where the hunters were butchering, it poured down upon us as if all the windows of Heaven had been at once unbarred. The lightening and the thunder, was dimming to the eye and deafening to the ear; and, withal, it was certainly just as cold as it could be without the water congealing. "I never saw it rain before," said a poor fellow, whose teeth were chattering together, in a manner that seemed to threaten the destruction of his masticators. "Nor I"—"nor I"—"nor I"—echoed half a dozen others, who were, as far as wet and cold were concerned, about in the same condition that they would have been, had they have been soaked an age in the Atlantic Ocean, and just hung out on the North Cape to dry. We made all possible haste; but, nevertheless, it was near two hours and growing quite dark, before we were ready to return to camp: and then we were so benumbed by the wet and cold, and encumbered with the meat which we had taken, that it was quite dark by the time we reached the River. When we came to the place where we had left the camp, we learned from one who had been waiting for us, that they had moved down the River, in hopes of finding wood. We therefore threw the remainder of our things, which had been left, upon our horses, and started to look for the camp. We saw our way by the lightning, and after traveling as we thought long enough to have gone several miles, we turned over the point of a hill, and saw a small light like that of a candle, away below us on the River. Taking a straight line for the light, we at length reached it, after having waded through a dozen sloughs up to our waists. We had expected to find a large blazing fire, and thought how comfortable we should be when we could warm and dry around it; and as we had not eaten any thing since morning, our apetites began to remind us how excellent a piece of roasted Buffalo meat would be. But how sadly were we disappointed, to find our companions shivering around a few coals, over which for fuel there was only a heap of green Willow brush. Wet, cold, and hungry, we spread our beds, which were of course as wet as water could make them, and turned in; but not to sleep—it was only to dodge the wind, and shiver the night away. At length the sky became clear, and the cold increased. We watched the stars, which seemed stationary in the sky. A dozen nights, according to the reckoning of our feelings, had time to have passed, and to us it appeared as though the sun would never rise; but at length it came, and never was dawn of day hailed more rapturously. One who was braver than the rest, summoning all his resolution, crawled out of bed: he would have leaped and ran, had he been able; but that was impossible.—His limbs refused to do their duty, and taking a hatchet, he waded across an arm of the River to an Island, upon which there was wood, and began cutting and carrying across. His example aroused others, and we soon had a large blazing fire. We spent several hours in putting our arms in order, drying our clothes and bedding, and appeasing our apetites on roasted ribs and marrow bones.

There were twenty of us, and we have frequently heard every one of that number say, afterwards, that they had seen some rough service in the world, but they had never met with any thing that could equal the night of the storm on the Platte. We continued to travel up the river, hunting as we went; but without much success. We saw a number of small herds of Buffalo; but they were generally too wild to approach, and too poor to eat after we had killed them. At the Forks, one hundred miles above where we first struck the River, we encamped, and by going several miles out beyond the hills, we succeeded in killing a number of Buffalo, the meat of which we brought in, dried and distributed among the company, when they came up; but the quantity was so small, in proportion to the numbers with whom it was to be divided, that it made scarcely a taste.

The Forks of the Platte is about the middle ground between the Pawnees and the Sioux. We saw a few of the Pawnees, in passing through their country, who were returning from the South, where they had been hunting, with packs of dried Buffalo meat, to their village, situated about fifty miles below where we struck the Platte. They are high, but well proportioned and active. They raise some corn, but live principally upon the Buffalo, and are the most notorious rascals any where East of the Rocky Mountains.

The valley immediately at the junction of the two Branches of the Platte, is nearly twenty miles wide, and a large portion of it has a good soil. After we had passed the Forks, we made several attempts to cross the South Branch, but always found the water too deep; and continued to travel up the South side, until we saw that it would be impossible for us to find a ford; when we stopped at a large Cotton Wood grove, eighty five miles above the Forks, having determined to construct boats. For this purpose we procured in the first place, a sufficient number of green Buffalo hides, and having sewed two of them together for each boat, we stretched them over the wagon beds as tight as we could, with the flesh side out, and then turned them up in the sun to dry; and when they became thoroughly dry, we covered them with tallow and ashes, in order to render them more impervious to the water. The boats being completed, we proceeded to cross the goods of the company. Each boat was manned by six men. Some waded or swam along side, while others pulled by a long rope which was attached forward. The River here was about a mile wide. In this way the goods were ferried over, and the empty wagons were drawn across by the teams a short distance below, where the River was wider and shallower. The crossing was effected in six days, and without any serious accident. We pessed here the fourth day of July. The country, as we advanced West, became more and more barren, until here it was little else than a desert: and between this point and where we first saw the Platte River, it receives no tributaries from the South.

Having crossed the South Fork, we turned across the higher dividing lands, and traveled one day North West twenty miles, to the North Fork, without water. After traveling up the North Fork sixty five miles, through a country still increasing in sterility, we came to what is called the Chimney. It is situated on the South side of the North Fork, three miles from the River. It is a conical hill, one hundred and fifty feet high; from the top of which, a peculiar irregular shaft rises to the same height—making the whole about three hundred feet. The base of the hill is elevated above the water in the River, about seventy-five feet. It is a hard earth, composed of sand and clay, and may be seen for twenty or thirty miles. There are here several ranges of detached Sand Hills, running parallel with the River, the sides of which are almost perpendicular, destitute of vegetation, and so washed by the rains of thousands of years, as to present, at a distance, the appearance of Cities, Temples, Castles, Towers, Palaces, and every variety of great and magnificent structures.

On the 9th of July we had a splendid prospect of these Sand Hills. A dark cloud arose in the West, and the whole region was illumined by the reflected rays of the Sun, which, mellowed by its effect, had lost their dazzling power; and the prospect was softened, until it seemed one vast brilliant picture, wrought with a mysteriously magic touch. Beneath the rising cloud was a vast plain, bounded only by the distant horizon. Here and there, upon its surface, there arose splendid edifices, like beautiful white marble, fashioned in the style of every age and country, canopied by the clouds; yet gilded and flooded by the mellowed light of the mid day Sun. It was so beautiful, that it could not be lost while it lasted, and though the gathering clouds threatened to drench us with their contents, we nevertheless continued to gaze until the beautiful illusion passed away.

Late in the evening of the same day, we encamped by a fine Spring, at the foot of Scott's Bluffs, a range of high Sand Hills, which run into the River. They receive their name from a melancholy circumstance, which happened at them, several years ago.—A small party of Trappers were returning from the Mountains, to their homes in Missouri. Owing to the hostility of the Indians who inhabited the country, (the Sioux,) it was necessary for their safety, that they should not be seen. To prevent this, required the greatest precaution in their movements. A few days before they reached this place, one of their number, named Scott, was taken sick and continued to grow worse, until he was unable to proceed. His companions carried him to these bluffs, and supposing that he could not recover, they left him. Others passing that way, some years after, found his bones a short distance from where he had been left. From this circumstance, these hills have been called, since that time, after the name of that unfortunate adventurer. In the extreme point of these hills, near the River, and about fifty feet above high water, are found great numbers of semi-petrified Turtles, from one to two feet across, imbedded in the sand, and many of them entirely perfect. There are no animals of this kind now in the Platte River, or elsewhere in the country, for several hundred miles around.

We continued up the North Fork, and on the 13th came to Lauramie Fork, opposite Fort Lauramie. Finding it full, we were obliged to ferry, and for this purpose we procured two small boats from the Forts, lashed them together, and covered them with a platform made of wagon beds, which we had taken to pieces for the purpose. Upon this platform, we placed the loaded wagons by hand, and although the stream was very rapid, all succeeded in crossing without much difficulty. A few hours after we crossed, a hail storm came up from the North West; before which, our animals ran for several miles, over the hills. Fort Lauramie belongs to the American Fur Company, and is built for a protection against the Indians. The occupants of the Fort, who have been long there, being mostly French and having married wives of the Sioux, do not now apprehend any danger. The Fort is built of Dobies, (unburnt bricks.) A wall of six feet in thickness and fifteen in height, encloses an area of one hundred and fifty feet square. Within and around the wall, are the buildings, constructed of the same material. Those are a Trading House, Ware Houses for storing goods and skins, Shops and Dwellings for the Traders and

Men. In the centre, is a large open area. A portion of the enclosed space is cut off by a partition wall, forming a carell, (enclosure,) for the animals belonging to the Fort. About one mile below Fort Laurimie, is Fort Platte; which is built of the same materials and in the same manner, and belongs to a private Trading Company.

On the morning of the 16th, we left the Forts, and after having traveled ten miles, we came to the Black Hills, and encamped at a large Spring, the water of which was quite warm. The road through these hills is, of necessity, very circuitous; winding about as it must, to avoid the steeps, ravines, and rocks. They are very barren and some of them are high. On Long's Peak, which rises to the South, we could see a small spot of snow. We found in places, a few trees of Pine and Cedar scattered over the hills; but they were all small and quite dwarfish. We crossed a number of Creeks on our way through the Black Hills, in the narrow bottom lands of which, we generally found good grass for our animals.

On the 20th, we met Messrs. Vasques and Walker, with a company of twenty or thirty men, coming down from the Mountains, where Messrs. Vasques and Bridger have a small Trading Post among the Shoshonee or Snake Indians. They were loaded with furs and skins, which they were taking to the Forts on the Platte, where they supply themselves with such articles as they want for the Indian trade.

Eighty miles above Fort Lauramie, we came to the Red Butes, (isolated hills.) They occupy a space of many miles in extent, and a large portion of the earth and stone of which they are composed, is as red as blood.

On the 23d, we crossed the North Fork, one hundred and twenty seven miles above Fort Lauramie, and for two days after leaving it, we suffered considerably for the want of water—the little which we found, being strongly impregnated with a kind of Salt, prevalent almost every where in the neighborhood of the waters of the Platte. At one of these Salt Springs, there are numerous sinks, into wihch the Buffalo sometimes fall and perish, The surfaces of them are dry, and appear firm; but in many places, they would mire a man, so that it would be impossible for him to extricate himself or escape, without assistance.

On the 25th, we came to the Willow Springs, where we found a beautiful Spring, of very clear cold water, rising in a little green valley, through which its waters flow about one mile, and sink in the sand. We also found here, an abundance of Willow wood.—The hunters, who had been out while we were traveling, had seen several bands of Buffalo; and as they were the first we had met with since we left the South Fork, we remained in camp nearly a day, in order to recruit our stock of provisions. The great scarcity of the Buffalo, through this country—a circumstance which afterwards was the cause of much suffering to the Emigrants—was attributable, in a great degree, to the presence of Sir William Stewart, with his pleasure party, and fifty or sixty fine horses for the chase; who, while we were passing through the Buffalo country, constantly kept several days ahead of us—running, killing and driving the game out of our reach. It was cheap sport to them, but dear to us; and we were led to conclude, that, if ever again an English or Scottish nobleman sees fit to look for pleasure in the Rocky Mountains, while an emigrating party is passing over them, it will be prudent to place him in the rear, instead of the van.

On the 20th, we encamped on Sweet Water, one of the tributaries of the North Fork, near the Independence Rock; which is a huge isolated mass of coarse granite, about three-fourths of a mile in circumference, one hundred feet high, rather oblong, and rounded on the top. On the South side, next to the stream, which runs within ten yards of its base, it is almost covered with the names of different persons, who have traveled through this country. It was called Independence Rock, by Mr. Wm. Sublet, an old Indian Trader; who, several years ago, celebrated here, the 4th of July.—These masses of detached and barren rocks, extend many miles up Sweet Water, principally on the North side. At the Sweet Water Canion, about four miles above the Independence Rock, the river runs half a mile through a narrow chasm, between rugged and almost perpendicular walls of rock, which rise on either side to the height of about three hundred feet,—(and this constitutes what is known through the Rocky Mountains, Oregon and California, as a Canion.) Being informed by those who were acquainted with the country, that we should soon leave the Buffalo region, all the different companies of the Emigration remained several days on this part of Sweet Water, to procure provisions for the remainder of the journey. Owing to the scarcity of game, we were compelled to travel a day, and sometimes further, from the road, to find it. We made up a party here from our company, to go to the Mountains on the South, which were distant about fifteen miles from the

River. Having crossed over the plain, and seeing but few Buffalo, and those we saw being very wild, and some of the bands being already persued by other hunters; we continued along the Mountain to the farther extremity of the valley, and finding nothing here, we held a council, to decide what course it was best to pursue.—Differing in opinion, the larger number turned back to follow the base of the Mountain on the North side, while a small party continued on, intending to cross over it. We found it very steep, rugged, and difficult of ascent; and night overtaking us near the summit, we were compelled to encamp. The Mountain was covered in places with pine, and there were many small streams running down its sides, upon which there was an abundance of grass. The night was quite cold; but as we were in a deep sink, at the source of one of these Mountain streams, we thought there would be little danger of being seen, and built up a large fire; by which we slept very comfortably; having, before going to rest, tied our animals on the grass. In the morning we ascended to the summit, to ascertain what lay beyond it, and look over the best probable field for game. Having gained it, we saw an extensive plain, through which, at a great distance, there was a River flowing, which we supposed to be the North Fork of the Platte. The descent to it was easy, and there were several bands of Buffalo feeding upon it, below us. We returned for our horses, and having passed into the plain, began to approach the nearest herd; but they took fright before we came within shooting distance, and we proceeded to the next. Having come near them, we stopped, leaving one of our company with the animals, while we approached nearer on foot. The ground favoring, we succeeded in bringing them within the range of the rifle; and killed three before they ran off. It was now the second day since we had eaten, and as soon as we could load our animals with the choice meat, we went to the nearest water, (which, contrary to the way it generally happens, was only a short distance from us,) kindled a fire and had a fine feast of "roasted ribs and marrow bones."

Having what meat we could carry, we proceeded West, along the foot of the Mountain, for a deep gap, which we had seen from the other side, in the evening. About sunset, as we were going along, we saw three Bears, up in the breaks of the Mountain, busily engaged scratching in the earth for roots. Having taken advantage of the ground, we approached near to them, and again leaving our partner, who was not a very good shot, a little distance behind with the horses and mules, we climbed up to the brink of the ridge between us and the Bears, and fired at the largest one. It fell, and supposing that we had given it a dead shot, we borrowed our companion's gun, intending to serve the second in the same way; but finding the first still alive, we gave him the contents of the second gun; upon receiving which, he sprang upon one of the others, and cuffed him until he squalled for dear life. We returned and were hastily reloading our rifles, and had only poured down the powder, when all three came rushing to the top of the hill, roaring most furiously, and so loud that the answering hills and hollow caves were filled with the beastly thunder. They stopped within forty yards of us, and in open view, rearing up on their hinder feet, the wounded one in the middle—which, as he stood, was about eight feet high—with the blood streaming from his mouth and down his side, snuffing the air on every side, to catch some tainted breath of us; but the wind was ours, and being blind with rage and pain, he did not discover us. Our companion became dreadfully frightened, so that he lost all reason, and commenced running around his horse, and exclaiming loudly, "Oh Lord! what shall we do?" We told him to mount; but he still continued running around his horse, bawling at the top of his voice; "Good God Almighty! what shall we do?" "Mount! mount!" said we again; but he paid no attention, and was making about the twentieth trip around his horse, crying aloud, "Oh Lord!" "Oh Lord!" at every step; when we gave a loud whoop, and the two Bears that were not wounded wheeled and ran off, and the wounded one tumbled back down the hill. This set our partner a little to rights, and turning to us, with a look of most perfect simplicity, he exclaimed, in a half weeping tone, "Good God! we can't fight them three Bears." You were frightened, were you not? said we. "O no, no, not bad scared," said he; "but stop—stop—look here," he continued, "may such another beautiful roar as that we just now heard, be my music from this on, if you ever catch me in a bear fight again," he added, shaking his head.

Having finished charging our rifles, and dispatching the wounded animal, we proceeded towards the gap, traveling until late in the night; when one of the mules throwing off and scattering its load, obliged us to encamp. The next morning we set out again, at the dawn of day, and soon reached the gap; which we found to be a deep break, extending entirely through the Mountain, and about two hundred yards wide. In passing through the gap, we came to several fine looking springs bursting out from the base of the Mountain; and dismounting to drink, we found them to be strong of Sulphur, and upon examining more closely, we saw the little cave out of which the largest one ran, in a stream about equal to the size of a man's arm, was entirely covered with a thick coat of crystalized Sulphur. The water was cold, slightly acid, and very pleasant. The country around is romantic, affords all the different varieties of game common in the Mountains, and would, we think, be an excellent resort for invalids, and persons of weak and disordered constitutions. The trip, the pure Mountain air, and the rough and wholesome manner of living, have already restored many who were before feeble and afflicted; to health, strengh, and activity; and we are convinced they are better remedies for constitutional or pulmonary diseases, than all the Patent Medicines and learned prescriptions, with which the public have ever been gulled.

Having passed through the gap, we traveled across the valley of Sweet Water, and to the trail of the Emigrants, and saw, from its size, that all the companies had passed. We hastened to overtake them, which we did that night; but not until late. During our absence, Messrs. Vasques and Walker came up, on their return from Fort Lauramie, and afterwards, traveled with us to their Trading House.

On the 1st of August, we saw arise from the horizon, like distant clouds, the snow crested summits of the Wind River Mountains. They are several miles North of the Grand Pass, and are one of the highest portions of the Rocky Mountain range.

On the 2nd, we made another hunting party, and proceeded again across the Mountain, on the South. After having gone about thirty miles from the trail, we saw a large band of Buffaloes; but, as it was late in the evening, we thought it best not to disturb them before morning. When morning came, not a Buffalo could be seen upon the plain. We hunted again all day, and in every direction, without finding any thing, and encamped at night in the Mountains, between where we were and Sweet Water. The third day, we went about fifteen miles further to the South, and saw a band of Buffaloes. We attempted to approach them; but they were so wild, that we could not get within a mile of them, before they would run. While following them, we saw an Indian, about half a mile off, and galloped towards him. At first, he fled; but finding that he could not escape, he stopped. When we came up, one of our party, (a Trader, belonging to the Company then traveling with us,) who understood his language, spoke to him. He was very much frightened when he saw that we knew he was a Sioux, expecting to be killed, on the spot, We asked him where his company were. He told us they were at a Lake, which was about three miles distant, making meat, and that they were three hundred in number. We turned to go away, when the Trader observed that we ought to kill him; but the rest of us objected, and he was overruled. Turning again to speak to him, he said he thought we had two hearts: one to kill him, and another to let him go; and that he did not know how to talk to us: that he did not know whether he should go under or not—(meaning that he did not know whether we did or did not intend to kill him.) But we turned away and left him, taking a straight course for the Company, thinking it not very safe to be in the neighborhood of three hundred Sioux. We put spurs to our horses, and kept a good gait, until we considered that we were out of their reach.

We arrived at our Company's encampment that night, having killed nothing. When we told them of our adventure with the Sioux, all the Traders joined in exclaiming against us, for not killing him. We plead that it was unmanly, and unfair, to take the life even of the meanest enemy, under such circumstances; but they adopted the Indian argument, and said that as we were among Indians, we must treat them as they treated us; and so the white people, who live in the Mountains, act towards their enemies.

On the evening of the 7th, we left the head of Sweet Water, and in a few hours passed over the dividing ridge, through the Grand Pass, and encamped by a marsh, which is one of the sources of Green River, a tributary of the Colerado, of the Gulf of California.

We slept here, on the great Backbone of North America, where the sources of the Rivers which empty into the Oceans which bound it, on the East and on the West, are only a few miles apart.

The lofty summits of the Wind River Mountains, with their wide fields of eternal snow, appeared to be almost beside us. We had a heavy frost during the night, and in the morning, the water in our camp kettles was covered with ice nearly one fourth of an inch thick; and every thing that had been exposed to the dew, which fell in the evening, was perfectly glazed with ice.

Both the ascent and descent, were so gradual, that, had we not been told, we should have passed over the dividing ridge, in the Rocky Mountains, without knowing it. The distance from our crossing of the North Fork of the Platte, to the summit of the Grand Pass, is one hundred and fifty four miles; and the country between, is a perfect desert.

CHAPTER II.

THE JOURNEY OUT, WITH ITS INCIDENTS.

Trading House of Vasques and Bridger—Attacked by the Sioux—Soda Springs—Deep Chasm and the Crater of an extinct Volcano—Fort Hall—Snake or Lewis River, Falls, &c.—Snow Storm, and difficulty of starting fire—Indians along Snake River—Numerous evidences of great Volcanic action in past times—Fort Boise—Hills of Marble—Grand Round—Blue Mountains, &c. —Whitman's Mission, on the Walawala—Fort Walawala—Columbia River, Falls, &c.—Cascade Mountains—Wascopin Methodist Mission—Indian Burying place—Fort Vancouver—Arrival at Oregon City, &c.

Having crossed the two Sandys, (branches of Green River,) on the 10th of August we crossed the main stream, a large and beautiful River; the water of which, unlike that on the opposite side of the Mountains, is very clear. Having crossed several of the tributaries of Green River, on the 13th we arrived at the Trading House of Messrs. Vasques & Bridger. It had been attacked, during their absence, by a band of Sioux; by whom the horse guard, and two Snake Indians, had been killed, and a number of horses driven off.

We remained here three days, and then went on to the Utah Mountains, at the head of Bear River, to hunt Elk; as our stock of provisions was nearly exhausted. We made our camp at the foot of the Mountain, where we remained ten days; during which time, the Utah Indians came to us, to trade horses, skins, &c. We met with but little success in hunting, and on the 28th started down the River.

On the 1st of September, it rained, was quite cold, and the hills were covered with snow. This day, we struck the trail of the Oregon Company, and during the nights we had heavy frosts. The valley of the River, is from one to eight miles wide. A large portion of it has a good soil, and is covered with an excellent grass. Flax grows spontaneously in this valley, and in considerable quantities. The hills on either side, rise very high, and are rugged and barren; and there are only a few Cotton Wood trees scattered along the River. These streams abound with a fine Fish, called the Mountain Trout. We found wild Goats, and large flocks of Geese, Ducks and Cranes; but they had been so much hunted, by the Emigrants, that it was almost impossible to kill any of them.

On the 4th we came to where the valley appeared to terminate,—the River turning short to the left, and making a breach through the high range of hills on the West; but the general course of Bear River is nearly North. Here we crossed over the hills, and again came into the valley beyond.

On the 7th, we reached the Soda Springs. They are on the East side of Bear River, and are scattered over a level space, about equal, in extent, to one square mile; with a slight inclination to the River, and elevated above it some fifteen feet. A large portion of this level space is covered with a stinted growth of Pine and Cedar. The earth is of various colors. In some places it is almost perfectly white, and in others, quite red, &c. Above, below, and on the opposite side of the River, the valley is rich, and covered with fine grass. The Mountains, on the North and East, are barren; but on the West, they are covered with Pine. The Springs, are deep pots in the earth, from one to fifteen feet across, and generally without an outlet. The water appears to be originally fresh, and seems to rise to a common level in all the Springs; and in these pools, which have been probably made by strong jets of the rising gass, it becomes highly charged. A slight hissing sound, is occasioned by the escapement of the gass. The water, in many of the Springs, where the surface exposed is small, is cool, very pleasant, and has a fine, pure and lively acid.

About half a mile below, and immediately on the bank of the River, there is a Spring where the water, (which is quite warm,) at intervals of fifteen seconds, is thrown several feet in the air, from the centre of a small conical rock, which it has formed about it. A few feet from where the water escapes, there is a hole in the rock, connected with the channel through which the water passes, which inhales and exhales the air, like an animal breathing. There are numbers of dried-up fountains, similar to this, back from the River, hollow truncated cones, from three to thirty feet in diameter. Several Springs rise in the bed of the River, the water of which is quite warm. Every thing here has the appearance of recent and powerful volcanic action, and doubtless the causes still exist, at no very great distance.

Five miles below the Soda Springs, the River makes an acute angle about a bold and lofty point, called the Sheep Rock, running away to the South West. Here, also, it seems to have made a breach through the Mountain, into another valley. Formerly, the Blackfeet Indians frequented this country; and, at this Rock, they had repeated battles with the Mountaineers, and with other tribes of Indians: and here the effects of their deadly encounters may still be seen, in bleached skulls and scattered bones. At this point, we left the River, and bore off to the right, across the valley, which is about ten miles wide. This valley appears to have been sunk several feet, and is full of chasms, from two to twenty feet wide, and of unknown depths. Volcanic rock is scattered over it, in large masses; and in many places, it appears to have been upheaved from beneath. We passed, on the left, a large, hollow mound, the crater of an extinguished Volcano.

It was late in the night before we reached the Western side of the valley, and found wood and water for our camp. The water upon which we encamped, was a branch of the Portneiff, a tributary of Snake or Lewis River. We noticed, scattered over the country, a kind of black volcanic glass, shaped like the fragments of a broken bottle. Winding our way through the hills, by a very circuitous route, on the 13th of September we arrived at Fort Hall. It is situated on the South bank of Snake River, in a rich valley, about twelve miles wide and twenty-five miles long, and in latitude about 43 deg. 20 min. North. The Portneiff, Black Foot, and many other small streams, run through this valley of Fort Hall. The streams are lined with a fine growth of Cotton Wood timber, and the entire valley abounds in excellent grass. The Company keep several hundred cattle and horses, at this place, which live through the winter, generally, without much attention. We were told by one of the members of the Company, that wheat had been sown at the Fort, and grew well. Fort Hall is built of the same material, and nearly in the same manner, as the Forts on the Platte are.

Leaving Fort Hall, we traveled down the South bank of Snake River, and a few miles below, we crossed the Portneiff, a beautiful little stream emptying into it; and at eighteen miles, came to the American Falls. Here, the River, compressed into about two thirds of its usual width, runs down, over rugged volcanic rock, a descent of about twenty-five feet in one hundred. The water is divided into three different shoots, by two large rocks on the Falls. In the middle shoot, there is scarcely any perpendicular fall; in the other two, there is about ten feet. Below these Falls, for many miles, the spurs of the Mountains, on the South side, run down to the river, and the road over them, is, in many places, steep and rocky. We crossed a number of small creeks, which run down from these Mountains to the River; the water of which, is cool and clear.— Many of the hills, over which we passed, were covered with a dwarfish growth of Cedar; and the Mountains on the South, with Pine. The River, below the Falls, runs through a deep and narrow Canion; between black and rugged basaltic walls, and is little else than a succession of Falls and Rapids.

The valley through which Snake River flows, is very wide, elevated from one to three hundred feet above the stream; and bounded, on the North and South, by parallel ranges of high Mountains. Its surface is broken, and cut by deep ravines. It is very sandy and barren, producing nothing but wild sage, and a few scattering blades of short grass. In traveling through this valley, it is necessary to obtain some directions, from those who are acquainted with the way, since grass is seldom found, except on the small streams.

A few days after our departure from Fort Hall, we left our camp one morning, when, according to our bill of the route, we had a long stretch ahead, before we would come to wood and water: the clouds were floating heavily along the sides of the distant Mountains; and the wind blowing in fitful gusts, made us fearful of an approaching storm. But our scanty supply of provisions induced us to proceed. We had not gone far, before the Heavens were completely obscured by the clouds. The cold increased to severity, and the mingled rain and snow, began to fall very fast. The dim trail, which led us over a high barren plain, became more and more indistinct, from the accumulating snow. The distant Mountains, already as white as the flakes that filled the air, gradually faded in the storm; and the extent of vision lessened, as it increased. We were drenched with the rain and snow, and chilled and pinched with the cold; and in vain did we attempt to excite warmth by walking: for, loaded down with wet garments, and being accustomed to remain mostly on horseback, we were soon fatigued with traveling, at a rapid rate, over the wet dust and sand, and began to fall behind. We went on for some hours, the storm still continuing; and the same gloomy prospect was still around us. We were ignorant how long we should have to endure the cold and fatigue, before we could reach some poor shelter; or whether we might not entirely loose our obscure path, and be compelled to pass the night without shelter or fire. We began unanimously to give expression to such fears, when we came suddenly upon the river, at a small grove of Willow bushes, and hastened to unload our animals and kindle fires. It was a long time before we succeeded in producing fire from the flint and steel; but, after many attempts, we at length obtained it, by sprinkling powder into the crown of a hat, together with whatever dry combustibles we could find, and discharging a pistol into it. To this we added the dry Willows which we had collected, and soon had a comfortable fire. We constructed frames of the green Willows, upon which we spread our blankets; and in this manner sheltered ourselves in some degree, from the snow and rain, which continued to fall during most of the night. The weather, previous to this, had been quite warm; and on the succeeding day, the clouds broke away, and it was again pleasant.

Eighty three miles below the American Falls, there is another tremendous perpendicular Fall in Snake River, over which the Salmon are unable to pass. Thirty-nine miles farther down, we saw, on the North side of the River, two very large Springs, bursting midway from the lofty precipices, rushing down like rivers, and foaming along over the piles of rock. They looked, at a distance, like banks of snow resting on the cliffs.

Seventeen miles below these Springs, are the Salmon Falls. These Falls are not perpendicular, except in one or two small shoots, on the North side. The great body of the water, runs down an inclination of not more than twenty-five feet in three hundred yards. The river here is about one hundred and fifty yards wide, and divided by an Island, commencing at the lower end of the inclination, and extending down one fourth of a mile. The Salmon pass over the Falls with ease, when there is sufficient water on them.—The surrounding country is very rough, broken, and entirely destitute of both grass and wood. The hills are, from the water in the River, about three hundred feet high. On the South side, they are cut up by ravines; but on the North, they come bold and unbroken, up within a few hundred yards of the water. There is nothing very picturesque or wild about these Falls, compared with the world of waste and wreck around them. The Indians take immense quantities of Salmon here; which they cut into thin slices, dry in the Sun, and afterwards pack them up, in grass cases. The natives, along Snake River, live principally upon fish and roots; and are the filthiest, most depraved, and degraded creatures, any where to be found among the dregs of human nature. We have been told, that during the Salmon season, they become as fat as penned pigs; and in the winter, so poor and feeble, that they frequently die from actual starvation.

After leaving the Salmon Falls, we traveled down near the river, our path frequently leading us along the sides of the almost perpendicular bluffs. Twenty-seven miles below the Salmon Falls, we came to the crossing; where the companies, which preceded us, had passed over to the North side, which is much the nearest and best way; but we, having attempted the crossing and finding it too deep, were obliged to continue down on the South. This is, perhaps, the most rugged, desert, and dreary country, between the Western borders of the United States, and the shores of the Pacific. It is nothing else, than a wild, rocky, barren wilderness, of wrecked and ruined Nature; a vast field of volcanic desolation.

Beyond the Mountains, which rise on the South of this point, is the great Salt Lake. Eighty-eight miles below the crossing of Snake River, we crossed two small branches of hot water. This region appears once to have been a high, level plain, which seems to have been overflowed from the East, by a vast flood of lava.— We were led to this conclusion, from noticing that the basaltic layer, which covers the surface of the hills, (the summit of the hills being nearly on the same level,) decreases in thickness, as we proceed down the River, until it gives out entirely; and the sandy base, which composes the hills, seems to have given away to the action of time, until these table hills are but the fragments of the vast wreck. In these deserts we found the Horned Toad, and a kind of Lizard, which is about eight inches in length, of a greyish color, slenderly proportioned, very swift, and apparently inoffensive.

Thirty-two miles below the Hot Branches, we crossed the Owyhe River, traveled down it two miles, and came opposite Fort Boisé, which is situated on the North side of Snake River, a short distance below the confluence of the Owyhe and Boisé; the latter of which, comes in from the North. There is, on the Boisé River, a great deal of Cotton Wood timber; from which circumstance, it takes its name. From the crossing of Snake River, to where it passes through the Blue Mountains, there seems to be no Falls or dangerous Rapids. At Fort Boisé, part of our company which came from Fort Hall, in hopes of procuring provisions, with the intention of going across into California, having obtained sm all supply, and the best directions they could get concerning the route, from Captain Payette, the principal at the Fort, (who appeared to be friendly, and much of a gentleman,) left us, to travel through a country, a large portion of which no white man had ever visited. They were to follow the Malheur, a small stream that empties into Snake River twelve miles below the Fort, to its source, and to pass over the California Mountains, to the head waters of the Sacramento.

Leaving Fort Boisé, we traveled twelve miles, and crossed the Malheur, where there are many Hot Springs, rising out of the bank of the stream. Twenty-three miles from the Malheur, we came to the Brulé or Burnt River, and traveled up it to its source leaving Snake River entirely. After striking the Brulé, the country gradually becomes less barren. We found on this stream, vast hills of Marble. The road, through these hills, is very crooked and rough. From the head of the Brulé, we came next to the valley of Powder River. Here, the aspect of the country changes rapidly. Leaving behind us the Sage and Sand, we find the hills and Mountains covered with Pines, and the little valleys along the Creeks and Rivers, with excellent grass. This valley is about ten miles wide, and thirty miles long; a large portion of which has a good soil. It is encircled by hills and Mountains.

Thirty-three miles from Powder River, we descend abruptly, some three thousand feet, into the Grand Round; which is a level plain, about ten miles wide, and twenty miles long, surrounded by Mountains, and traversed by the Grand Round River, which comes in from the West, runs nearly to the middle of the plain in several channels, joins with another branch, bears away to the left and leaves the plain at its Northern extremity, through a low gap.—Numerous small creeks and rivulets, run through all parts of the valley, from the surrounding Mountains. There are some Balm trees on the River, and the Mountains are covered with Pine.—Much the largest portion of the soil is very rich, and the whole is covered with a superior quality of grass. From the Grand Round we bore to the left, and began the assent of the Blue Mountains. It was long, but gradual. After reaching the summit, the road was generally passable, excepting some deep ravines, which were frequently very steep and rocky. A great portion of these Mountains, are covered with dense forests of lofty pine. Those portions which are destitute of timber, are generally covered with good grass, and a considerable portion of the soil appears to be fit for cultivation.

On the third day, we left the Mountains and descended to the Umatila or Utilla River, (generally called in that country, the Utilla,) in the valley of Walawala. From the brow of the Mountain, we had a fine view of the Cascade range, fifty miles distant, forming the Western boundary of the valley, stretching far to the North and South, with its lofty peaks of eternal snow rising among the clouds. The extent of the Walawala valley, is not known; but it is probably three hundred miles long, with an average width of about fifty miles. Its course, from and below the junction of Snake River, is nearly South; above, it bends away to the East. The Columbia River runs through it to the Dales; where it leaves the valley, and breaks through the Cascade Mountains. This valley, is elevated above the Columbia, from fifty to five hundred feet, and is very uneven, dry, sandy, and entirely unfit for cultivation, except along the base of the Mountains, and immediately on the smaller streams which run through it; the principal of which, are the Walawala, Umatila, John Days, and De Chutes Rivers. Almost the whole of the valley, is covered with a superior quality of grass; which springs up in the Fall, is green through the Winter and Spring, becomes cured in the latter part of Summer; and affords sufficient food for animals throughout the year. It grows in detached bunches; the blades are eight or nine inches long; and it is generally considered almost as nutritious as grain. With the exception of a few Cotton Wood trees on some of the streams, there is no timber in the valley; but there is an abundance on the neighboring Mountains. Lead has been found on the Umatila; but not, as yet, in any considerable quantities. This is the country of the Walawala Indians. They own a great many horses; some of them have as many as two thousand—and they are the finest Indian horses we have ever seen.

Thirty miles from the Umatila, we came to Whitman's Mission, situated on the Walawala River, twenty-five miles from its junction with the Columbia. The buildings are of unburnt brick, and are neatly and comfortably finished. The Missionaries have a Mill, and cultivate a small piece of ground.

We were told by Mr. Spaulding, the Superintendent of the Mission on Clear Water, distant about one hundred and fifty miles from Dr. Whitman's, and on the North side of Snake River; that, in the neighborhood of his Mission, as far as he was acquainted with the country, it contained many rich valleys, of considerable extent; and, from what we have been able to learn, from all the different sources of information with which we have been favored, it is our opinion, that that portion of country laying between Snake River and the main branch of the Columbia, will in the course of time, be inhabited by a civilized people; as it doubtless contains some good valleys of land. The country of the Spokines, laying on the Spokine River, is said to be good. That occupied by the Cour De Lion and Calespell Indians, contains many Lakes and Marshes. About Fort Colville, on the upper Columbia, the Hudson's Bay Company cultivate the soil, with good success. Snake River, from where it leaves the Blue Mountains, to its junction, is clear of Falls and Rapids.

From Dr. Whitman's Mission, we proceeded to Fort Walawala, situated on the East bank of the Columbia, at the mouth of the Walawala River. Here we disposed of our animals, procured canoes from the Indians, and having obtained a pilot from them, we cast our frail barks, on the waters of the Columbia. The River, up and down from the Fort, as far as we could see, was broad and smooth, and we promised ourselves an agreeable passage: but we soon found that it was full of rocks, whirlpools, and dangerous rapids; to follow through which, in safety, required the greatest exertion, watchfulness, and care. Our minds were constantly filled with anxiety and dread, and the wild manner in which our savage guide warned us of approaching danger, had no tendency to dispel our unpleasant feelings. On the first day after leaving the Fort, one of our canoes, in which there were three persons, one of whom was a lady, in passing through a narrow shoot in the Grand Rapids, struck a rock, upset, and filled instantly. The lady and her husband succeeded in gaining the rock; which was about three feet across the top, and just under the surface of the water. Our pilot succeeded in taking them off in safety, and regained most of the property. We passed on to what is called the Chutes, through many dangerous Rapids; to have accomplished which, would have been very impracticable, without skillful guidance. Here the River is wide, full of large rocks standing out of the water, and falls several feet. We were compelled to make a portage of nearly a mile, over the rocks and sand, carrying our canoes and baggage on our shoulders. Three miles below the Chutes, are the Little Dales; where the River runs three hundred yards through a narrow channel, between high rocks. Here we made another portage of our baggage, and smallest conoe, and with some difficulty hired the Indians to run the others through the rugged Canion. A few miles further, and we came to the Great Dales; where we were compelled to leave our smallest canoe, and again make a portage of our baggage, a distance of one and a half miles, over the rocks.— Here, the whole Columbia runs through a Canion not more than seventy feet wide, whirling and boiling in a most furious manner, running with terrible velocity, and chafing against its rugged, rocky walls; and it requires the most dexterous management, which these wild navigators are masters of, to pass the dreadful chasm in safety. A single stroke amiss, would be inevitable destruction. Three miles below the mouth of this Canion, and one hundred and twenty-five miles below Fort Walawala, is the Wascopin Methodist Mission, at this time under the superintendence of Mr. Perkins, and situated half a mile from the South bank of the River. They have a small Farm attached to the Mission, under the superintendence of Mr. Brewer. Both this and the Mission on the Walawala River, though they are well located, for the purposes for which they are intended, and conducted, perhaps, according to the best judgment of those who have charge of them; have not yet, we believe, been productive of much, if any, good. Here we were obliged to remain more than a day, on account of high wind, by which we were detained several days on our passage to the Cascade Falls. From the Mission to the Falls, a distance of fifty miles, the River has scarcely any current. The Mountains are high on either side, rocky, and in many places covered with heavy forests of Pine; some of which, are at least ten feet in diameter and three hundred feet high. A short distance below the Mission, we found the stumps of trees, standing erect, in ten or fifteen feet water, as if a dam had been thrown across the River, and the water backed up over its natural shores. We asked the Indians if they knew how these stumps came to occupy their present position; but none of them were able to inform us. They have a tradition among them, that long ago, the Columbia, in some part, ran under the ground; and that, during an eruption of Mount St. Helens, the bridge fell in. Some such circumstance as this, is the only way possible, in which this anomaly can be accounted for, unless Captain Fremont is correct, (which is certainly, extremely doubtful,) in supposing them to be land slides. For they are found no where below the Cascade Falls, although the character of the River, and its shores, is, above and below these Falls, very much alike. They are found immediately above the Falls, and as far up as the still water extends; which lack of current in the River, we consider to be the effect of some vast impediment, having been thrown into it, at the Cascade Falls. The Falls seem to be composed of large detached masses of rocks; which circumstance also favors our opinion. A short distance below the Wascopin Mission, and the Rapids of the Great Dales, we found the first of these submerged stumps. They increased in number, as we descended the River; as is always the case wherever there has been an impediment, thrown into the channel of a stream, so as to raise the water over its natural shores. Immediately above the Wascopin Mission, as we have before noticed, and at least as far up as Fort Walawala, the River is full of Falls and Rapids, and such also we believe to have been the original character of the River below; where we find, at the present time, these stumps, and an entire lack of current; as this portion of it includes the breach through the Cascade Mountains, the most rugged country, perhaps, through which the Columbia flows. If these stumps and trees, (for many of them are still sixty or seventy feet above the water in the River,) had been brought into their present position by land slides, as Captain Fremont suggests, it seems to us, to be a matter of course, that the most of those which were not throwh down by the motion, and agitation, would have been found standing in various inclined positions; but on the contrary, we find them nearly all standing erect.—And again, what is highly improbable, the slides must all have been very nearly simultaneous, as the trees are all, about in the same state of preservation. The most of them stand opposite where we considered the shores too gradual to admit of a slide. There are many large nooks in the Mountains, along this part of the River, which are suitable for small settlements.

Fifty miles below the Mission we came to the Cascade Falls.—Here the River, compressed into two thirds of its usual width, descends over huge rocks, several hundred yards, with an inclination of about five degrees; and from the head to the foot of the Rapids, a distance of four miles, the water descends about fifty feet. From the great agitation of the water, caused by its rushing with such velocity, down its rocky channel, the surface of the River, for several hundred yards, is as white as a field of snow.—On the South, the dark basaltic walls, rising perpendicularly four or five hundred feet, are covered with Pines. There are small Islands of rock, both above and below the Falls; many of which are timbered, and huge volcanic fragments cover either shore. Here we were obliged to leave our canoes, and carry our baggage nearly four miles, over rocks, and hills, to the foot of the Rapids; where we found a bateau, which had been brought up from the Fort, for the accommodation of the Emigrants.

We saw, while passing down, on the North side of the river, a large Indian burying place, where the bones of hundreds were heaped together, in pens about eight feet square, made of thin Cedar slabs, hewn and set upon end in the earth, covered with bark, and ornamented with carved images of birds, beasts, skeletons of men and imaginary monsters. Some of these pens had rotted down, and the naked skeletons lay scattered over the ground. We found in one, a body not yet decayed, wrapped in a blanket, and laying upon a board shelf.

The Falls afford one of the best Salmon fisheries in the Territory, and here the Indians take, in the Spring, great quantities of fish. It rained on us during the night we were at the Falls, and, with little intermission, during our passage to Vancouver. Below the Falls on the South side, there is, for several miles, a perpendicular rock bluff, rising from the water five hundred feet; over which several small streams are pouring, in beautiful Cascades. The Columbia is broad and deep from the Falls to the Ocean, and the tide runs up to the foot of the Rapids. Twenty miles below the Cascades, the River makes a sudden bend, about a high Mountain point, colled Cape Horn. Immediately on the point, there are several spires of solid rock, rising, like huge horns, out of the water, from fifty to sixty feet high. Here we were met by a heavy gale of wind, and compelled to run ashore, and remain until the next day. This frequently happens to voyagers, on this part of the River. In one instance, a crew of Emigrants were under the necessity of throwing part of their loading overboard, in order to gain the shore. A few miles below Cape Horn, the highlands on the South side, recede from the River, leaving wide, low bottoms; which generally overflow in the Spring. This low land continues to widen, to the mouth of the Willammette, and extends up that River about eight miles. In this part of the Columbia, there are many low Islands.

After a very disagreeable passage, we landed at Fort Vancouver, forty miles below the Cascade Falls. It is situated on the North side of the River, one hundred miles above its mouth. The buildings occupied as stores, warehouses, shops, residences of the agents, men, &c., make quite a village. The ground back, for half a mile, is level; and then rises, with a gradual inclination, until it is elevated several hundred feet above the River. It is set with grass, and makes a very pretty appearance. Vessels drawing fifteen feet water, ascend the Columbia this far, without any difficulty. Vancouver is the principal depot of the Hudson's Bay Fur Company, West of the Rocky Mountains. Their furs are collected from all parts of the Territory, to this place, and shipped once every year, to England; and the vessel returning, brings, annually, a cargo of goods, to supply the trade. They keep constantly on hand, one year's supply in advance, that if any accident should happen to the vessel, either on her outward or homeward bound passage, the trade might not be interrupted.—The Company have some good farms, and several large herds of cattle and hogs, in different places. They have an extensive dairy, on Sophia's Island, at the mouth of the Willammette; where they make, annually, several thousand pounds of butter and cheese; which they send to Sitka, a Russian settlement, to the North, with which the Hudson's Bay Company have also a contract to furnish a large amount of wheat, yearly. In return for which, they are to receive the Russian furs. They likewise furnish the Sandwich Islands, with a considerable amount of flour, lumber, spars, and fish; for which they receive, in return, the products of those Southern Islands. The great design of this Company, is to trade with the Indians, and take the beaver; but, after this animal, so unfortunate on account of the rich dress which Providence has given it, as a shield against the cold of the North, had become nearly extinct, in the lower valley of the Columbia; and after the settlement of foreigners in the Sandwich Islands, and citizens of the United States in Oregon, began to create markets, they extended their operations, and began to cultivate the soil, to raise cattle, to build mills, to furnish the settlers with articles of merchandize, and to trade with foreign ports.

Having obtained a skiff at the Fort, belonging to Oregon City, we went down the River six miles, to the upper mouth of the Willammette. The lower mouth comes into the Columbia twenty miles below, making Sophia's Island. The hills are very high on the West side of the River; but rise gradually, and are covered with dense forests of Pine. We had but little difficulty in ascending the Willammette, there being not much current until we came within one and a half miles of the Falls, where we found a strong Rapid, at the junction of the Clackamus; a small, but rapid River, coming in from the East. Here we were obliged to get out into the water, and draw our boat by a cord, several hundred yards.

Having passed these Rapids, we arrived, in a few minutes, at Oregon City, situated at the Falls of the Willammette, the place of our destination. This was the 13th of November, 1843, and it was five months and nineteen days after we left Independence, in Missouri. Here we were able to procure such things as were really necessary to make us comfortable; and, what was most especially pleasing to us, an abundance of substantial food. We enjoyed that plenty which, until now, we had long been strangers to; and were happy, after a long and tedious tour, over mountains and deserts, through a wild and savage wilderness, to witness, upon these distant shores, the home of Civilization : To see houses, farms, mills, store-houses, shops; to hear the busy hum of industry; the noise of the workman's hammer; the sound of the woodman's axe; the crash of the falling pines; and to enjoy the warm welcome of countrymen and friends. How grateful these circumstances were to us, he who has never passed the bounds of Civilization, or forsaken the parental roof, can never know. We had been here but a short time, before the last of the Emigrants arrived. They were soon scattered over the country. Those who intended to cultivate the soil, laid claims, built cabins, and prepared for the coming winter. Mechanics found employment at the Falls, and those who had no particular occupation, or object in view, distributed themselves through the country, taking hold of whatever circumstances offered, or suited their inclinations best. All found enough to do, and there was in the country, an abundance of the real necessaries of life. Every one seemed satisfied, for a time, with being permitted to have a home and a plentiful subsistence.— And notwithstanding many were greatly exposed, during the winter season, all were blessed with excellent health.

Our arrival had a great effect upon the country. The people were beginning to feel lonesome, and to fear that it would be long before these far distant wilds of Western America, would be settled. Property was of doubtful value, and their once high anticipations were fading away. They had heard reports from the Indians, of the approach of a great number of white people; but the reports were disbelieved, and we were our own heralds; for, not until we arrived, were they convinced of our coming. Instantly every thing revived; improvements went rapidly on, and the expectations of the people were again excited. We found, at the Falls, a small village of about one hundred inhabitants. Lots were laid out on both sides of the River; those on the East side, by Dr. McLaughlin, Chief Factor of the Hudson's Bay Company, West of the Mountains. and called Oregon City; those on the West, by H Burns, and Called Multnomah.

CHAPTER III.

DESCRIPTION OF WESTERN OREGON.

Willammette Falls, Mills, &c.—Description of the Willammette Valley—Head of the Willammette River—Calapooiah Mountains—Umqua Valley—Umqua Mountains—Valley of Rogue's River—Clamuth or Chesty Valley—Description of Country North of the Columbia—Mount St. Helens, an active Volcano—Numerous low Islands in the Columbia River—Astoria or Fort George—Indians West of the Cascade Mountains—their method of catching Salmon—Government organized—Peopling of America and Pacific Islands—Scenery in Oregon.

Great improvements were made in the little Town, at the Falls of the Willammette, during our stay in the Country. There was, at the Falls, when we left, a Saw and Grist Mill on one of the Rock Islands, belonging to an American Company, styled the Oregon Milling Company, and on the main shore, two Saw Mills and a large Merchant Flouring [illegible], belonging to Dr. McLaughlin, four Dry Goods Stores, a School House, two Churches, a Public Library, a flourishing [illegible] Society, Law offices, Physicians, Shops, and Mechanics of almost every description, and a population of about three [illegible] persons.

At the Falls, the Willammette precipitates down a perpendicular basaltic rock, thirty-three feet, and spreads out as it approaches the precipice, into a broad sheet, at the verge of which it is nearly a half a mile wide. It is divided by two large Islands of rock, into three different shoots. The whole descent of the water from the level surface above, to that below, is about forty-five feet. The River for some distance above and below the Falls, runs through a channel cut in the solid rock. On the East side, extending down from the Falls several hundred yards, and back from the water five hundred and fifty feet, there is a perpendicular wall, one hundred and fifty feet high; further down, the space between the hills and the River, increases in width, until there is sufficient room for a town of considerable size.

The Valley of the Willammette, which has generally been considered the best portion of Oregon, is situated on the South side of the Columbia River, between the Cascade Mountains, a lofty range running nearly parallel with the coast, at a distance from it of about one hundred and twenty-five miles, and the Calapooiah Mountains, a range of considerable height, which rise immediately on the coast, and extend along it so as to form an entire rock bound shore. The Valley has an average width of about seventy-five miles, and extends South one hundred and fifty miles. It is traversed from South to North, by the Willammette River, a large and beautiful stream, which is navigable to the Falls, within two miles of which the tide reaches. The Falls overcome, and navigation reaches fifty miles further up the River. This valley is divided into several portions, by ranges of high lands running in different directions, generally following the course of the streams. The principal tributaries of the Willammette, are the Clackamus, which rises in the Cascade Mountains and empties one and a half miles below the Falls; the Twalita, which rises in the Calapooiah Mountains, flows through the Twalita Plains, and empties two miles above the Falls; and, eight miles above the Falls, the Moolally or Pudding River, which rises in the Cascade Mountains and empties into the Willammette, from the East: fifteen miles above the Moolally, the Yamhill River, which empties from the West; and above the Yamhill, the Sandy Yam, which empties from the East. The streams emptying from either side, have their sources in the bordering Mountains. On the lower Willammette, the country near the River is broken, and covered with dense forests of Pine. Further back from the River, it is diversified, with open woodland and groves of heavy timber; and still further, there are beautiful plains, lying between the streams, separated by belts of timber, and extending back to the Mountains. On the upper Willammette, the country is more open and level, and is diversified with groves af Oak, Pine, and Fir, and broad and fertile plains, covered with luxuriant crops of grass. Above the mouth of the Yamhill River, a range of hills commences, and follows the Willammette River, continuing, gradually, to increase in height, to its junction with the Columbia. From the mouth of the Willammette, they follow the South bank of the Columbia, within fifteen miles of the Ocean; thence they bear away to the South, and join with the Calapooiah Mountains, at Cape Look Out, twenty miles South of the Columbia; encircling the Twalita plains, a cluster of small, but rich and beautiful prairies, lying twenty miles West of the Falls of the Willammette, being in extent, about equal to thirty miles square and connected by the Shohalam Valley and Yamhill district, with the upper Willammette. In the upper Willammette Valley, the plains are more extensive, and in some places, there is a scarcity of timber; but the soil is fine, and frequently we meet with small spots of clover, growing wild, over many parts of the country.—Seventy-five miles above the mouth of the Sandy Yam, the Willammette Valley rapidly decreases in width, until it is nothing more than a narrow defile, between the Mountains. No one has ever traced the River to its source, and but little is known of it, beyond the head of the Valley. It has generally been thought to rise in Mount McLaughlin, one of the highest peaks in the Cascade range, and it is so marked, on the best maps that have been made of the country; but the information we have received, from the Company which went across, from Fort Boisé to California, convinces us to the contrary. They stated, that, after leaving the waters of Snake River, and ascending a high Mountain, they came upon an extensive level table land, which they supposed to be about eighty miles across, having a good soil, and being diversified with forest and plain; and that, having obtained an Indian pilot, whose language they could not understand, it was with much difficulty, they persuaded him, that they wished to go to the South West. The Indian showing them a small stream, and pointing to the North West, informed them that it led to a settlement of people, similar to themselves, and they were convinced that their guide alluded to the settlement on the Willammette, and that this was its source.—They finally succeeded in getting him to understand that they were aware of the location of the settlement, to which he alluded, and that they did not wish to go to it. After reflecting some time, the Indian seemed to recollect, like a dream, of there being white people to the South West, and accordingly conducted them to the head waters of the Sacramento, which has its sources, as they informed us, in the Southern part of this same table land.

The country on the Eastern side of the Willammette, is very similar to that on the West, excpting that it is rather more level, and not so high, or uneven, near the River, and is not separated from the Columbia, by any high range of hills, as it is on the Western side. There is an abundance of excellent timber in this valley, the greatest portion of which is Fir. There are, also, in different parts, considerable quantities of Oak, Pine, and Cedar; and besides these, there is Hemlock, Yew, Balm, Maple, Alder

Laurel, Dogwood, Cherry, and Ash, with a great variety of shrubs, and plants; and many such as we have never seen in any other country. Besides the power at the Falls of the Willammette, which is alone sufficient to propel an immense machinery, there is a vast amount of the water power, in this valley; at least entirely sufficient, always to supply every want of the country. Besides the Mills at the Falls, of which we have already made mention, there are in the upper Willammette, a Grist and Saw Mill, belonging to the Catholic Mission, and a Grist and Saw Mill, built by the Methodist Mission, and another Saw Mill building by an individual. In the Twalita plains, there is a Flouring Mill in operation, and a Saw Mill in progress of building. Seven miles above Vancouver, the Hudson's Bay Company have Saw and Grist Mills. Twenty five miles above Astoria, and near the Columbia, there is an excellent Saw Mill in operation, and on the Clatsop plains, there is a small Patent Mill being set up for the accommodation of the settlers, at the mouth of the River. The present population of the country, the great portion of which is in the Willammette Valley, amounts to about 6000 souls (exclusive of the Natives.) A portion of these are English, French and half breeds; but a large majority are from the United States, and have emigrated to this country over land, within the last four years. Those who have come into the country, have been industrious, and improvements have gone rapidly on. Quite a considerable portion of the Willammette Valley, has already been brought into cultivation, and there is, after supplying the inhabitants, and emigration, annually, several thousand bushels of surplus wheat. New farms are being opened daily, and the cabin of the bold and enterprising pioneer, may be seen rising on many a verdant hill, or nestled away in the quiet seclusion of many a flowery nook; and ere long, the plow share and the axe promise to turn this wild and flowery wilderness into rustling fields, and blooming gardens.

The Valley of the Umqua is divided from that of the Willammette by the Calapooiah Mountains, a single and almost unbroken ridge, the course of which is nearly East and West. Across these Mountains, which are not high, and the ascent and descent of which are very gradual, is a distance of about twelve miles.—They are thickly covered with good Fir timber, are not rocky, and have a soil fit for cultivation. The Umqua Valley is about thirty five miles wide, and its length is not certainly known. Its general character is very similar to the Willammette Valley, excepting that its surface is more undulating. The Umqua River runs through the middle of the Valley, receiving numerous tributaries, from the neighboring Mountains. It is a stream sufficiently large for navigation; but the great rapidity of its current, will probably always prevent it from being useful for that purpose.—The Valley is diversified with woodland and prairies; but the prairies occupy the greater portion, the timber being principally along the water courses and on the bordering Mountains. The prairies have a good soil, and are covered with a most excellent kind of grass. There is a great deal of fall in the smaller streams; and, having their sources in the Mountains, they are constant, and afford numerous fine water privileges. There is some granite in this Valley; but the prevailing rock is basaltic. The Umqua Indians, are quite numerous. They are not openly hostile to the whites; but yet, it is not considered entirely safe, for a few persons to travel through their country. No settlement has yet been made in the Valley, and no person has yet visited it, except those passing through, to or from California. The Hudson's Bay Company have a Trading Post near the mouth of the River. Supplies are taken to it over land, from Vancouver, on pack animals. There is a small bay at the mouth of the Umqua; but the depth of water, at the entrance, is sufficient only for small vessels. It affords a tolerable harbor; but the intervening Mountains, extending along the coast, separate the Valley from the Ocean, and the River passing through them, probably contains Falls, Rapids, and Canions, that will prevent vessels from passing any considerable distance up the River. This Valley, although it is separated by the surrounding Mountains, not only from all other portions of the country, but also from the Sea-board; nevertheless, offers sufficient inducements, to ensure its speedy settlement. The Calapooiah Mountains are so gradual and unbroken, that a good waggon road can easily be made across them, into the Willammette Valley, and a rail road can be made, to connect it with the navigable waters of the Willammette, whenever the necessities of the country require it, and its wealth is sufficient to construct it.

South of the Valley of the Umqua, are the Umqua Mountains, running nearly parallel with the Calapooiah Mountains, and separating this Valley from the Valley of Rogue's River.—The distance across them is fourteen miles. They are high, very steep, and somewhat broken; but not rocky, and covered with forests of Fir, so dense, that they entirely prevent the growth of grass.

South of this range is the Valley of Rogue's River, having the same course with the Valley of the Umqua, and being about twenty-five miles wide. Its general character is much like that of the Umqua; but it is more level, has a soil of a rather better quality, and is also covered with good grass. On the North side, where the California trail crosses the Valley, it is principally wooded; on the South, Prairie. Immediately above, the proportion of prairie and timber is very good. Here, as in the Umqua Valley, the timber is on the streams, and the prairies are between them. There is, in the Valley, quite a considerable quantity of granite; but basaltic is the most prevalent rock. The Valley appears to widen above: its length is not known. It is traversed by Rogue's River; a stream somewhat larger than the Umqua, and not so rapid but that it might probably be made useful for transportation. Salmon ascend the River in great numbers; and so do they indeed, most of the streams throughout the whole territory of Oregon. Water power is not wanting in the Valley of Rogue's River. A few miles below the California trail, the River appears to enter a Canion, and the Mountains along the coast are high and rugged; so as to prevent advantageous communication with the Sea-board. The Indians who inhabit this Valley are numerous, and almost in a state of nature. They are of small stature; but well proportioned—slender, active, and sensible. They have never had any intercourse, of consequence, with the whites, and have, therefore, but few of the articles manufactured by a civilized people. From their extreme hostility and treachery, and from the great amount of damage they have done to the white man, they have been almost universally called the Rascals. They seldom allow a company to pass, without molestation. They attack from ambuscades, made in defiles, chasms, and thickets. They have no fire arms; their principal weapons being the bow an arrow. Their bows are made of the wood of the Yew tree; short, and covered on the back with the sinews from the loins of the Elk, which are fastened on with glue, and neatly and securely wrapped at the ends with the same material. Their arrows are feathered, and pointed with small, delicate, uniform and very sharp heads of flint. These arrows they shoot with great force and precision. They seldom have horses, and if they take or kill an animal in their attacks, (which they endeavor to do as much as to take the lives of the men,) they afterwards cook and eat it, making a great feast.

South of the Rogue's River Valley, is the Chesty Mountain, a single, and almost bald and barren ridge. To the right of the California trail, it bears a little to the South, and interlocks with the Mountains on the coast. The Northern base is covered with timber; the summit and Southern side, in many places, with large boulders of granite. The distance across is six miles. Going towards the South, the ascent is gradual—the descent rather steep; but a very good road might be made across, into the Clamuth or Chesty Valley, which lies immediately South of the Chesty Mountain, and has nearly the same course with the Valleys of the Umqua and Rogue's River. This Valley of the Clamuth is about thirty miles wide, where the California trail crosses it. It decreases in width below, and increases above. It is traversed by the Clamuth River; a stream still larger than Rogue's River; but full of rocks, rapids, and narrows; and passing through the Mountains of the coast, it appears to run through a narrow Canion, affording no outlet from the Valley to the Pacific. The soil of this valley, is generally of a very inferior quality; but along the streams, and at the foot of the Mountains, it is good. The rest is a kind of dry, light, dusty and sandy land, producing but little vegetation. The surface of the Valley, is generally quite level, and a large portion of it is open. There are a few scattering Oaks, in places through it, and some Pine; but the timber is, principally, the Fir growing along at the base, and on the sides of the Mountains. The Clamuth Indians are numerous, and quite hostile. Their character and condition is much the same as that of the Rascals. This Valley is situated near the parallel of 42 deg., and we are not certain whether it is in Oregon, or California.

These Southern Valleys of Oregon, though in their present state of nature, so lonely, so wild, and so secluded: though they now threaten the travelers who pass, at intervals of years, with dangers from the rugged mountain path, the swollen torrent, and the savage arrow: though many a gloomy glen, and rocky gorge, and dark and tangled wood, which have been stained with conflict, or storied by some savage ambuscade, still stand to awaken terror in the passer by; yet, these Valleys, notwithstanding their wildness and dangers, offer inducements, (deadly to the fated native,) for which, ere long, the stronger hand of the white man will beat back the present wild and implacable inhabitants, and make them the homes of civilization. Each of these Valleys, is probably of sufficient extent to make several large counties; and, but for their detached position, and their being so separated from the sea-board as they are, or appear to be, they would doubtless be the most desirable part of the Oregon Territory. The general fertility of the soil, is favorable to the agriculturist; the richness of the grasses, to the stock raiser; the vast beds and piles of stone, and the broad forests of the giant Fir, to the mechanic; while the unfailing abundance of water in the Rivers and creeks, pouring over numerous falls and rapids, present inducements highly favorable to the manufacturer. Occupying a position between where the Winter rains of Oregon, and the Summer droughts of California, are occasionally severe; they possess a climate, which, mingling these two opposite evils, destroys them, and thus renders these secluded Valleys, in this respect, the most desirable portion of these most desirable climes. But they are so much as nature made them, and so wild, that many portions of them have never been trodden by the foot of the white man; and it may be, when time, and the bold enterprise of our Western adventurers, shall develop, more fully, the character and resources of these mountain-wrapped solitudes, that there may be found a Pass, which nature has provided as a way for commerce through her barriers; and from the sides of the mountains, and from the bosom of the plains, may be drawn additional materials, to add to the necessaries and comforts of man, and to aid the march of civilization. It is possible that this portion of Oregon, will be acquired from the natives, in the same manner that portions of the United States have already been acquired—by force. And should it be so acquired, and when judgment comes upon the conqueror for conquest, there will be none upon whom it will fall more lightly! for there are no people who deserve more justly, punishment for "all manner of wickedness," than the natives of the Rogue's River and Clamuth Valleys.

Not much attention has yet been paid to the North side of the Columbia, by American settlers, owing to the uncertainty in regard to the claims of the two Powers, that hold it in dispute; but notwithstanding this uncertainty, a small settlement has been formed by persons from the United States, about twenty miles above Vancouver, on the North side of the River, in the confident belief that the United States Government would never relinquish any portion of her just rights. In several respects it is superior to the South. Immediately on the River, it affords many more, and better siutations for settlement. At the Falls of the Columbia, which must, in time, become a place of some importance, the North side only, can be improved. As the navigation extends forty miles above the Falls, and entirely through the Cascade Mountains, over which a good road cannot probably be made; a canal around the Falls will be a project which will deeply interest that whole country, as it will probably be the only means to facilitate the intercourse, between the different portions of country lying above and below the Cascade Mountains, and the ingress and egress from and to the United States; and a canal can only be made, with any reasonable expense, on the North side. The vast amount of water power which the Falls will afford, can be rendered available with profit, only on the North side. Cape Disappointment, which can be made almost as impregnable as the Rock of Gibraltar, and which entirely commands the entrance of the River, frowning down on the channel which washes its base, is also on the North side.

Puget's Sound, which is cut by the parallel of 49 deg., and is said to be surrounded by a very beautiful country, of considerable extent; in point of spaciousness, safety and facility of access, is the second harbor on the Western shores of America. The general character of the country is similar to that on the South, excepting that its valleys are not so large, and the mountainous and hilly portions, occupy a greater extent. Like the Valley of Willammette, the Valleys on the North side of the Columbia, are diversified with forest and plain. There is little or no difference in the soil, and the grass is equally fine. On the streams that empty into the Columbia, and their tributaries, there are many Falls and Cascades; which afford excellent sites for machinery, to an almost unlimited extent. On the Cawlitz, which is the largest falling into the Columbia from the North, below the Cascade Mountains, the Hudson's Bay Company have a Saw Mill, and there is, at the same place, a small French settlement, which has been connected with them; but their term of service having expired, they were permitted by the Company to remain in the country, (the contract of the Company with them is to return them at the expiration of their term of service, to their own countries. This is done in order to prevent competition.) They are engaged in agriculture, and furnish, annually, several thousand bushels of wheat, to supply the Russian contract. Their wheat is boated down the Cawlitz, in bateaus; but the rapidity of the stream, renders the navigation difficult and tedious. This settlement is fifty miles above the mouth of the stream. The valley, here, is not half so large as that of the Willammette; but it is, nevertheless, entirely sufficient to accommodate quite large settlements. There are many other smaller streams, emptying into the Columbia from the North; on all of which there are Valleys back from the River. The timber is more abundant on the North, and of rather a better quality.

Twenty-five miles North from Vancouver, and about opposite the mouth of the Willammette, Mount St. Helens, a lofty snow capped Volcano rises from the plain, and is now burning. Frequently, the huge columns of black smoke may be seen, suddenly bursting from its crater, at the distance of thirty or forty miles.—The crater is on the South side, below the summit. The Cawlitz River has its source in Mount St. Helens.

On the Columbia, in most places, the hills, which are generally high, frequently steep and broken, and covered with dense forests, come in on both sides, close to the water; leaving only small bottoms in the bends of the stream. Some of these bottoms, however, are large enough for several good farms. On the North side, for many miles above and below Vancouver, the bottoms are of considerable width. The hills are low, and rise gradually back, for some miles, affording room for large settlements. At the mouth of the Columbia, on the South side, is the Clatsop plain, extending along the coast; and from a mere point, at the Southern extremity, it increases in width, until it reaches the River, where it is about five miles wide. This plain is very sandy, and produces fine garden vegetables; but is fit for little else. It has probably been made by the deposites of the Columbia, thrown back by the waves of the Ocean. It is traversed by several sand ridges, like waves, running exactly parallel with the coast. As the Columbia approaches its mouth, it widens out ito broad bays; which, excepting a single channel, are full of shallows and sand bars; many of which are entirely bare at low tide.

About twenty miles above Astoria, there is a large cluster of low Islands, called the Catalammet Islands, several miles in extent; which are covered with Cotton Wood and Willows, and are overflowed by high tide. They are several hundred in number, and are separated by as many shallow channels; some of which, are as wide as the main channel: and into which, persons who were not acquainted with the River, have frequently run, and have been lost among the shallows for many hours. A few miles below these Islands, on the North side, there is a singular Rock, standing immediately in the channel, and rising above high water about twenty feet. It appears, at a distance, like an artificial Pillar, and has been called Pillar Rock. A few miles below this Pillar, the River is fifteen miles wide; and the channel, leaving the North side, bears across in nearly a straight line, to Tongue Point, which is several hundred feet high, extending out into the River, in the shape of a tongue, about half a mile; and commandidg, most perfectly, the channel which washes its base.

Astoria, situated on the South side of the Columbia, twelve miles above its mouth, is generally known as being the first place which was settled on that River. It contains only a few houses, and is occupied as a Trading Post, by the Hudson's Bay Company, and now called by them Fort George. Some of the hearth stones of the old Trading House of Mr. Astor, may still be seen. This will probably eventually be the principal commercial place in Oregon; as it is the best situation between Tongue Point and the mouth of River, and as there are on the bar, at Tongue Point, only three fathoms water, while on the bar at the mouth there are five. The River, at the mouth, is four miles wide, and the entrance is obstructed by a large bar, upon which the waves of the Ocean, (excepting in the channel,) break with great violence.—The flying sheets of foam may be seen from Astoria, and the roaring may be heard for a much greater distance. The point of land on the South is low and sandy, and is called Point Adams; that on the North, is a high, perpendicular rock, and as heretofore said, is called Cape Disappointment. The channel comes around close to the foot of the rock, so that it has entire command of that entrance of the River. Since the wreck of the Peacock upon these breakers, this entrance has been considered by many, in the States, as extremely dangerous; but not so with those who are acquainted with the channel. All admit, however, that it is necessary to have a fair wind, and weather sufficiently clear to observe the land marks, to avoid danger, as the channel is narrow. With these, together with a correct knowledge of the place, we doubt not but that a thousand vessels, were they sailed by men of skill and judgment, might enter the mouth of the Columbia, and not one be lost. In the case of the Peacock; it is said, that the Captain mistook the bar for the channel, and struck before he discovered his mistake. We believe that strongly constructed and powerful tow boats, directed by experienced pilots, would overcome this obstruction as effectually, as the same means do that at the mouth of the Mississippi. When vessels have accomplished an entrance, they find a safe harbor, and good anchorage, in Baker's Bay, just within

Cape Disappointment; and farther up, above, below, and opposite Astoria—in the main Channel of the River. The bad character which the mouth of the Columbia gained, by the unfortunate accident which happened to Lieutenant Wilkes, then Commander of the United States Exploring Squadron, in the Pacific, has since affected, materially, and deeply, the prosperity of that infant Colony: and not the Colony alone, but also the interests of the numerous Whalers, which are, in every direction, in every latitude and longitude, constantly traversing the broad bosom of this Ocean of Oceans; since it has certainly been the great cause, to discourage an intercourse, which would otherwise have been commenced, and carried on, to the great advantage of both. This character, which has been and still is so extremely detrimental, is, in a great degree, unmerited and incorrect.

The coast South, from Cape Look Out, (twenty miles South of the mouth of the Columbia,) to the Umqua, is generally rugged and mountainous. There are some small Valleys, on the intermediate streams; but none of sufficient extent to demand attention. At Cape Look Out, which is a lofty and frowning rock, extending into the sea, there are extensive sands, and a vast rock rising out of the water, called Kilamoox Head; upon which, when the wind is high from the West, the Ocean waves dash and break in such fury, that the roaring may be distinctly heard in the Willammette Valley.

The Indians, West of the Cascade Mountains, are divided into numerous small bands, and many of them without any acknowledged head. There were once, on the waters of the Columbia, the Willammette, and along the shores of the Ocean, powerful tribes; but pestilence and disease, since the coming of the white man, have swept them rapidly away; until but a few, poor, wretched, degraded beings, beyond the reach of charity, remain. Once Chenamus, a proud, intelligent, and influential Chief, of the Chenooks, held sway over all the tribes, between the shores of the Pacific and the Cascades, and between the Umqua and Puget's Sound; and extended his influence beyond the Mountains. But, after his death, his place was never filled: and now, the bones of his people, are scattered upon the rocks and hills, and their dwelling places, are their graves. The bones of hundreds, perhaps thousands, lay heaped up promiscuously, together. And every isolated rock that rises out of the Columbia, is covered with the canoes of the dead. They are nearly all gone, and disease is still sweeping the miserable remnant away; so that, in a few more years, there will not be a single red man west of the Cascades, on the waters of the Columbia.

The Indians of this lower country, are generally smaller, and not so well formed as the generality of tho Natives of America. They have but few horses, travel mostly in their canoes, and live upon fish, fowls, and roots. Their houses are constructed of slabs split out of Cedar, hewn, and set upon end, around a frame of poles, and covered with bark. The Indians are very filthy in their habits, and almost destitute of clothing. The stench arising from the filth about their villages, in the fishing season, is almost insupportable. They are superior water-men, manage their canoes with the greatest dexterity, and are very expert in fishing. On the Columbia, they fish with seins, (such as are used in the United States.) At the Falls, they build scaffolds, out from the rocks, near to the falling water, and use a sort of dip net, fastened on a long staff. They use spears, where a sein cannot be drawn; and in the night, they fish with hooks fastened on a pole, which they immerse deep into the water, and when they feel any thing touch the pole, they jerk it up quickly and generally bring out a fish. This mode of fishing is practiced only during the season in which the Salmon are ascending the streams, and immediatly below some great waterfall, where they collect in immense numbers. All the fish that are exported from Oregon, are caught by the Indians. Their canoes are the finest we ever saw; they are made of the large white Cedar, hewn out with great labor. They are constructed with a high bow and stern, which are separate from the main vessel, and so neatly put on, that the joints will not admit water.—They are very light, and the edges are ornamented with Sea shells. These people are also ingenious in the manufacture of mats of rushes, and hats and baskets of grass. Some of their baskets are water tight, and many of them are ornamented with devices of beasts, birds, and flowers, worked in various colors. The religion of these Indians, is much the same as that of the other tribes of America. They believe in one Superior Presiding Influence, which they call the Great High Chief. They believe also, in an Evil Spirit, and in numerous inferior Spirits, both good and evil, which inhabit the earth and air, and are invisible, or assume the form of smoke or vapor: the evil Spirits afflicting mankind with misfortunes, disease and death. They also believe in the Spiritualization of beasts, birds and fish, and even of their clothes, ornaments, canoes, tools, implements of war, &c.; of fruits, flowers, and numerous other inanimate things; and we are inclined to the belief that they extend this Spiritualization, to all organized bodies. It is on account of this opinion, that they bury their dead in their canoes, with many of the articles which belonged to them, while living—such as arms, clothing, ornaments, &c.—and furnish them with a supply of food, which they suppose sufficient to last them to the Spirit Land. For the same reason, a horse, or a dog, is frequently butchered beside the grave of a hunter. The Spirits of all of which things, according to their opinion, will be required for their comfort and subsistence, when they themselves have come to be disembodied Spirits. They are in many respects, very superstitious: One instance of which is shown, in the removal of a large stone which lay in the way of some men who were taking saw-logs into the River, a mile below Oregon City. The workmen were about to remove it, when they were forbidden by some of the Indians, and told that it was once a man, and if they removed it, the River would rise up to it. They, however, removed it; and it happened, that soon after, the River rose higher than it had ever been known; which accidental circumstance, was attributed by them to the removal of the stone, and of course, strengthened their superstition. They have what they term Medicine-men, in whom they place great confidence, and suppose that they possess the power, by means of charms, to counteract the influence of evil Spirits, and to drive them away. They are called to exercise their charms in every case of sickness. They blow their breath upon the body, rub it, and press upon the stomach. After continuing this for some time, they pretented to have drawn something from the patient; they press it in their hands, and appear to hold it with the greatest difficulty; immerse it in the water, and continue alternately to rub and immerse it, until the evil Spirit is overpowered. Then, holding the clenched hands above the head, several loud shouts are uttered in as frightful a manner as they are able. They then open their fingers gradually, to allow the terrified Scocum, (evil spirit,) to make his escape —blow through their hands—continue to utter fearful cries, and to make threatening gestures—until they have driven the agent of evil, entirely away. They go through the same operation, until they have drawn the last little devil from the body of the patient, and driven it away. All the time these incantations are going on, a number of persons sitting in a row beside the sick, chanting their savage song, beat constantly and loudly with sticks upon a large dry board. These Medicine-men are supposed to be invulnerable, and lead the van to battle. They frequently exhibit proofs of their magic powers, at their dances and celebrations, by holding live coals of fire between their fingers, for several minutes at a time. They are held accountable for the success of anything which they undertake, and if a person dies in their hands, or if they loose an engagement, they are tried for their lives. When a Chief, or member of a Chief's family, or other notable person dies, they are placed in their canoes, with their blankets, arms and other implements, which they used while living; hung to the bough of a tree, or placed upon a rock, and a favorite horse, and sometimes several slaves, are killed, to bear the soul of the dead to the world of Spirits. Slavery exists in the lower country.

These Indians are great gamblers, and they have several games, the form of which we are not able correctly to describe. They play until all their property is gone, and then frequently gamble off their bodies, part at a time, until the whole is lost, and they are slaves for life. Marriage, among the Indians, is rather a mercenary transaction, than otherwise. It is true, perhaps, that there is a choice in some instances; but generally, whoever pays the highest price, takes the woman. Poligamy is universally practiced, and some of the Chiefs have as many as ten wives. The wealth of an individual, is estimated frequently, by the number of his wives. The women here, as well as with all other barbarous tribes and nations, do all the hard labor; hunting, fishing and war, being the only duties of the man. But the Indians between the Umqua and Puget's Sound, are at this time any thing else but warlike. The time no doubt has been, when they were; but they have degenerated as fast as they have decereased in numbers, until they have, in every sense of the terms, become inactive and feeble. Perhaps no where on the great American Continent, on either side of the Isthmus of Panama, has their intercourse with the white man been more ruinous to them, than it has here. It is, however, no less strange than true and deplorable, that wherever the white man has had intercourse with the Indian, almost without an exception, it has tended both morally and physically to degrade, sink, and destroy him. The different tribes, differ from each other very much, in their language. They have not a great many words, and almost every one is uttered with a strong guttural sound. They count to ten, and afterwards, by tens and hundreds. These are the Flathead Indians, and we believe the only Tribe that prac tice this singular custom, upon the Continent of America, or upon the surface of the globe. How it has happened that the name has been given to a Tribe inhabiting the country upon the upper part of that branch of the Columbia, commonly known in the States by the name of Clarke's River, and separated, by several hundred miles, from the only people who are known to have ever practiced this custom, we are unable to imagine. Some ignorance and mistake, however, have thus widely misplaced the name : and instead of having given it to those whose most unnatural fancy would have rendered it highly appropriate, they have wrongly designated by it, a people whose heads are as round as our own. The same error has likewise been committed, in giving to a Tribe inhabiting a country on the North side of Snake River, the name of Nez Pierce, to whom the custom of piercing the nose is not at all peculiar; but which is practiced extensively by the Tribes along the coast; all of whom, are separated from these, who bear the name, by a distance of two or three hundred miles; and between whom the lofty range of the Cascade Mountains, (which intervenes,) admits but little intercourse. The custom of piercing the nose, for the purpose of wearing in it, shells, quills, rings, &c., is practiced somewhat, by all the aboriginal inhabitants of America. But with the Tribes, inhabiting these shores of the Pacific, it has been almost universal, and is still so with some. With those, however, who have had much intercourse with the whites, this, together with the custom of flattening the head, is beginning to be less observed.

The custom of flattening the head, originated, probably, in the idea, that it was unbecoming the dignity of a master, to wear the same appearance as the slave; and as garbs and insignia were perishable, or subject to be wrested from them, it seems that they determined to put on different, and, of course, as they were superior, more beautiful heads. And perhaps the circumstance, that their slaves were to accompany them, and serve them in another world—the land of spirits—was considered by them an additional reason, why they should imprint indelibly, even on their very existence, a sure indication, and record of their own superiority : lest, perchance the master might be mistaken for the slave, and to the slave might be awarded the privileges of the master : lest the proud master, who, in this world, was accustomed to grant his servant life, or bid him die, might, by mistake, in Heaven be compelled, himself, to suffer and to serve; might be compelled to dig the spirit-roots, and gather spirit-berries, from the bogs and briers of heaven; and to bare around the Portages or paddle along the Rivers, the ghost of his own, nobleman's canoe, for a vile slave: lest, in the fair land of spirits, his free-born shade might be, through mistake, compelled to bare such like ignoble spirit burthens, and toil, and sweat, and tremble, at the will of a vile creature of the Great High Chief of Spirits, whom he before had been accustomed to command: Lest such misfortunes might come upon him, by the too great natural resemblance, between himself and his slave, it is probable that he was more strongly induced to lay aside the servile-looking head, which silly nature gave him, and put on a more beautiful one of his own wise fashioning. If this be not correct, it is at least surely very much in the character of man; and if it be, it is not confined to the Flatheads, alone, nor is it peculiar to the ignorant and uncultivated barbarian. The actions of civilized and enlightened barbarians, speak with the same import. This operation of flattening the head, is performed when the child is very young: while the cranium is yet soft, and somewhat pliable. It nevertheless requires a long time to complete it. It must be effected very gradually, and the pressure must be continued upon the skull, until it has acquired a degree of hardness, sufficient to retain the shape which has been given. The object is to press back the forehead; which, when the operation is completed, is generally about parallel with the nose. In effecting this, the back part of the head is also somewhat compressed. This object is accomplished by binding a small board, or any other hard plane substance, closely upon the forehead; so as to press in the required direction. The child itself is lashed to a board, in such a manner, as to favor the securing of the flattening plane, in the necessary position, and to prevent the child from strangling. This operation, although so unnatural, so confining, and affecting an organ so delicate as the brain; and though performed upon such tender years, does not, however, appear to produce pain. Mortality does not appear to be greater among the Flathead children than among the adults, in comparison with that of other Indian Tribes. Neither does the flattening of the head appear, in the least degree, to affect the mind. Slaves, born among them, whose heads are not flattened, are the same, in every respect, pertaining to the mind, as far as it is possible to determine. In disposition, passion, intellect, and in their whole character, as far as different individuals are alike, they are alike But it is proba ble that this practice will soon become extinct, if not from the abandonment of the custom, at least from the extinction of the race.

In the climate of Western Oregon, we find one of the principal advantages which this country, together with the whole Western coast of the Continent, possesses over those portions laying East of the great mountain range, which, extending from within the Arctic circle, along the whole extent of North and South America, to Cape Horn, divides the Continent into two Grand Divisions, different, not only in their geographical features, but also in climate and vegetation. The climate of Western Oregon is milder by several degrees, than it is between the same parallels of latitude in the States. Snow seldom falls in the Valleys South of the Columbia, and during our stay at the Falls of the Willammette, which embraced two Winter seasons, there were only two falls of snow; (with equal and perhaps greater propriety, we might call that portion of the year included between the first or middle of November, and the last of March, the rainy season;) the first of these snows was six or eight inches deep, and remained upon the ground about three days; the second, which continued to fall at intervals, during a week, passed away almost as fast as it fell, never concealing, entirely, the surface of the ground. During the period of our stay, we never saw ice on any of the streams of water; yet, it has been stated that since the location of the Hudson's Bay Company at Fort Vancouver, the Columbia River has been twice closed over at that place. If this be a fact, it must be owing, in a great measure, to the circumstance that the Columbia has its sources in far Northern latitudes, and in high mountainous regions. On the Willammette which flows from the South, such congelation has never been known. We were informed by persons, long resident in the country, that rains were very frequent through the Winter or rainy season, but that great quantities seldom fell in short times. During the first Winter we were in the country, there were several weeks together, of fine, clear, and most delightful weather, and besides this, several other shorter periods of cessation; but during the second, it rained almost constantly, yet so light were these rains, generally, that in order to convey correct ideas, propriety would seem to demand some other term to designate them. Taking the two seasons together, which we experienced there, we doubt whether a greater quantity of water fell than falls generally in the same length of time, during the same months in the States.—

Many have expressed objections to the climate, on account of the rainy seasons, and it cannot be denied that they frequently render it quite disagreeable and gloomy, especially to those who have just emigrated to the country. Yet most persons do their accustomed business at this season, whether it be in or out of doors, without seeming to experience any great inconvenience, or suffering detriment to their health. Southern winds prevail in tne Willammette Valley, at this season, and when they change to the North they are usually succeeded by fine, clear weather. At the same time, however, they prevail from the East or change to the West on the Columbia, showing their course is effected very much, by the hills and mountains. The clouds float low in the Winter, and frequently huge masses of them, as if influenced by attraction, cling to the sides of the hills and mountains, until as they move along, they are torn by the tops of the tall Firs. We saw once as we were laying becalmed on the Columbia, in the dusk of the evening, the clouds descend from the mountain ravines, and settle down, for awhile, so near the surface of the broad river, that the Islands with which it was there interspersed, and portions of the neighboring shores which were covered with groups of tall trees, penetrated with their tops, above the cloud. Their seeming to be much elevated, together with the regularity of the upper surface of the cloud, awakened the idea of a beautiful little Archipelago, with all its Islands, floating in the air. The grass is green and growing throughout the Winter, and cattle and other animals keep in good condition, without any attention or feeding whatever, and we have frequently eaten excellent beef, killed from the grass at this season. In the Summer, there is probably not so much rain, as in the United States; but it is entirely sufficient to perfect the crops of grain, which, except Indian Corn, are more abundant, and surer, than in the United States. The temperature at this season, is near the the same that it is in the same latitude East of the Mountains, except the nights, which are quite cool during the whole year; so that a person may sleep in mid summer, comfortably under a pair of blankets. These cool nights are doubtles injurious to the growth of Indian Corn, which does not flourish and produce abundantly in this country. The sky, through the Summer, is usually clear, and on the plains, a gentle breeze is generally blowing from the sea; which renders the Summers remarkably agreeable and healthy. The natural vegetation of the country, is all of a giant growth. We have spoken of the Fir's attaining to the height of three hundred feet; many others, of the smaller kinds of vegetation, are in the same proportion. We have seen the common Elder growing from six to twelve inches in diameter, and the Hazle very commonly from four to six inches. There are several different kinds of wild fruit in the country, which are not found in the United States, and several which are, though it is not more abundant here than in the States. The cultivated fruits common in the States, such as the apple, peach, and pear, appear to come to perfection; though but little attention has yet been paid to grafting and cultivation; consequently, there is but little fruit of a good quality. The grape, although not a native of Oregon, and not found any where West of the Rocky Mountains, and North of 42 deg., in a wild state, having been planted at Vancouver, is said to produce well. The wheat grown in Oregon is of a very superior quality: the grain is larger, fuller, heavier, and in every way finer, than that grown in the States. The quantity produced, with the same cultivation, on the same extent of ground, we also think, is something more; but the difference is greater in quality, than in quantity. The varieties of forest trees are not great; the Pine, Fir, White Cedar, Hemlock, and Oak, being the principal. There are also, some Maple, Ash, Alder, Dogwood, and Cherry, found along the watercourses. Thunder is seldom heard West of the Cascade Mountains, and storms and heavy winds are not prevalent. The Territory of Oregon has with great propriety been considered in three divisions. These divisions are natural and strongly marked, not only by the mountain ranges which separate them, but also, by difference in soil and climate, and of course by different degrees of productiveness, and by a different general appearance. That portion of the Territory lying between these mountain ranges, (the Cascade and Blue Mountains,) is, under the above division, the middle portion, but is generally known in that country under the name of the Walawala Valley. Under this name we have previously noticed it, and thus we will designate this division, wherever it comes, in the course of our remarks. The climate of the Walawala Valley differs from that of Western Oregon, in being much dryer and somewhat colder. It appears strange that between two portions of country situated in the same latitude, and separated only by a range of mountains, the difference of climate should be so marked. We will not pretend to account for this difference, but will suggest that the elevation of the Walawala Valley above the Valleys of Western Oregon, together with the circumstance of its being much farther from the Ocean, and separated from its influence, by a very lofty range of mountains, might make the difference. This climate, together with the dry and sandy character of the greater portion of the soil, and the richness of the grasses which they produce, renders this portion of Oregon, above all others highly favorable to grazing; and it is in our opinion, especially adapted, on these accounts, to the raising of sheep. As we have before remarked, the grass springs up here also, in Autumn, and is green, and frequently growing, through the Winter: so that animals require no other food. The almost entire absence of timber in the Walawala Valley, is attributable to the dry and sandy nature, and to the insufficiency of the soil. The few Cotton Wood and Willow trees which line the margins of some of streams and Rivers, and the Pines which grow at the base of the Mountains, is all the timber which the Valley affords. Where the soil along the streams and near the mountains is rich; the climate fovors the production of wheat, rye, oats, &c.; the common garden vegetables; and is supposed to be more congenial to the growth of Indian corn, than that of Western Oregon. Corn has been grown for some years, in small quantities, at Dr. Whitman's Mission, and some of the Walawala Indians have been induced to cultivate small patches of it. But the ears we saw were small, and the quantity produced has also been small; and we are confident of our correctness in saying, that there is no portion of Oregon in which this grain can be profitably produced. The climate of the Walawala Valley, and every thing else connected with it; the dryness of its soil, the purity of its waters, and the vicinity of snow covered peaks, are certainly highly fauorable to health; and in proof of its healthfulness, we have the testimony of those who have resided in it as Traders, or Missionaries, for a number of years; and not only the testimony of words, but also of appearance.

The remaining portion of the Territory of Oregon—the Eastern portion—we have sufficiently noticed, in passing through it. Very much the largest portion of Eastern Oregon, is at present, and must continue for a great number of years, to be, comparatively valueless. It is a desert, so rugged, so dreary, and so exceedingly sterile, that it cannot, until ages upon ages have melted its mountains; until the winds, and floods, and changes of thousands and thousands of years, shall have crumbled into dust, its rocks, and its sands; yield anything worthy of consideration, to the support of human life. There are, however, some beautiful exceptions to this general character; bright and blooming valleys, walled with mountains, and surrounded by wastes; which, contrasting so widely with every thing about them, are regarded by the lonely traveler, as being, not only wildly romantic, but surpassingly beautiful. These however, are rare. The traveler through that dreary region, will climb to the summit of many a barren height, and traverse many a sun scorched plain, ere the green Oasis glads his eyes.

Those who have emigrated to the country, have had uncommonly good health. Notwithstanding the great exposures which the Emigrations of 1843 and 1844, were necessarily subjected to, in making, and after having made, a long and toilsome journey through a wild, and desert wilderness; in preparing shelters from the rains, and obtaining the means of subsistance; there were fewer instances of sickness in either, than is common among a like number of people, in the most healthy portions of the United States. But to describe the climate of Oregon, with the greatest exactness, in the fewest words, is, we think, to compare it with France; which laying between precisely the same parallels of latitude, and occupying exactly the same position, on the Eastern Continent, that Oregon does on the Western, boasts a climate which has long since and universally been acknowledged, one of the finest on the Globe.—The situation of Oregon, in regard to commerce, every one who knows any thing about the geography of the world, is already acquainted with. Its location is convenient to all the shores and Islands of the Pacific, the Western portions of South America; and as all the numerous groups of Islands in the great Pacific Ocean, are ready of access; they will furnish much for profitable commerce, as they lie mostly in the tropics.

The people who have emigrated to Oregon, have organized a Government, deeming it right and necessary, situated as they were, in an Indian country, and so far removed from the influence of any law; not only as a means of personal safety from the natives, if they were disposed to be hostile; but also, for the protection of life and property, against evil-doers among themselves; and for the distribution of equal justice in all their intercourse with each other. This Government, however, is intended only to be temporary, and subject to the disposition of the Government of the United States, whenever she extends her jurisdiction over the Territory. The people of Oregon, generally, have no disposition to set up an independent government; but on the contrary, they are exceedingly anxious to be taken into the care and under the protection of the United States. They expect to receive grants from the government, and under this expectation, they have all located land claims of a section each; and these claims are of course respected and protected by the existing provisionary government. This government was organized in 1843, and previous to the arrival of our Emigration. The citizens met in Convention, and elected an Executive Committee of three, which had the powers of a Governor, a Legislative Committee of nine, a Judge, Recorder, Treasurer, Sheriff, four Justices of Peace, and as many Constables. Military Officers were also elected, and several companies of Militia organized. They made a short code of written Laws, defining the duties and powers of the different officers, and adopted the Laws of Iowa so far as they would apply to their condition. They regulated the taking of land claims, determining who might hold claims, and defining what steps should be necessary, in order that persons might be secure in the possession of lands. They limited these land claims by the same authority by which they laid them, (Senator Lynn's Bill,) to six hundred and forty acres, and made any person laying two claims, liable to loose either. In order to hold a claim, they made it necessary that the corners of the land, should be marked; and that a description of it should be entered upon the books of the Territorial Recorder; and the temporary government agreed to protect these land claims against all other claimants, except the United States of America. The Missionaries residing in the Willammette valley, who took an active part in the organization; besides the claims allowed them as individuals, succeeded in obtaining, in the name of the Mission, thirty six square miles; and in the best portion of the Willammette Valley. The succeeding Legislature, however, disregarded it; and all except the usual claim allowed to individuals, was liable to be taken by any one who might wish it. This government was extended over all the country between the parallels of 42 deg. and 54 deg. 40 min. North latitude, and West of the Rocky Mountains to the Pacific Ocean; and made a residence of six months necessary to Citizenship. The second Legislature, elected by order of the Executive Committee, made a Law, prohibiting the making and selling ardent spirits, in the Territory, except for Medical purposes; and likewise, a Law prohibiting the residence of negroes in the country, after the expiration of three years; and levied a tax upon the people, for the construction of roads, and the defraying of expenses unavoidable, in the transaction of the Government.—They have endeavored to protect the rights of the Indians, and promote peace and harmony between them and the settlers; and no disturbance of a genral nature has ever occurred between them; and an Indian war, in all probability, will never interrupt the tranquility of the Willammette Valley. The temporary government is acknowledged and supported by the great majority of of the people, and is constantly gaining strength and character.—None of the members of the Hudson's Bay Company took an active part in the organization of this Government; yet we believe that Dr. McLaughlin was present at the Convention.—Since, however, many of those persons whom the Hudson's Bay Company have settled in the country, have been induced, by the influence of members of the Company, to vote at elections.—Many of the individuals connected with the Company, among whom is Dr. McLaughlin himself, have preferred to avail themselves of the benefit of the Laws, to become subject to them, and to pay the taxes levied by the Legislative Committee. One of the officers of the Hudson's Bay Company was appointed by the Executive, to the office of Treasurer of the temporary Government, and he accepted and served in that capacity. But little difficulty has yet occurred in its administration, and only two instances of resistance against the Laws; in both of which, the authorities were successful, and order was maintained. Private difficulties have but seldom occurred, and there is more harmony in society than we have ever known or heard of, in any other part of the world.—This happy circumstance is attributed principally, to the general absence of intoxicating liquors; which is a state of things unprecedented in the settlement of a new country, and speaks loudly in favor of the moral character of the people of Oregon.

Many speculations have been indulged in, since the first discovery of America, much research made, and many opinions offered as to the manner in which it became peopled. We have, in the course of our travels, become acquainted with some facts which may possibly throw light upon this subject. It may be, that the facts which have induced us to form our opinion, have been given to the public by others, and long since; but if they have, as we have never seen them, we beg leave to throw our opinion into the scale. The most commonly received opinion, is, we believe, that the first inhabitants came across from the Northern part of Asia, at Berring's Straits, where the distance between the shores of the two Continents is but short. This opinion, though it is very plausible, and in fact, probable, as regards America, cannot account for the peopling of many of the Islands in the Pacific Ocean, far removed from the shores of either Continent. It is our opinion, that the Western shores, if not the Continent of America, and all the inhabited Islands of the Pacific, have been peopled from China and Japan. It is now known, with as much certainty, as are any existences or transactions, of which we have been informed, by ancient history, that the Chinese Empire has been in existence, that its people have been in many respects enlightened, and that records have been made and kept by them, for several thousand years past. They had vessels in which they went to sea, but not having an extensive knowledge of navigation, they never ventured far from land; it however, sometimes happened, that they were blown off to a great distance, at sea, became lost and bewildered, and were left to the mercy of the wind and waves; in this condition, we believe that these lost vessels have been driven and cast upon the shores of our Continent, and upon the inhabited Islands of the Pacific, where the people who thus saved themselves, have increased, and made the aborigines of this Continent, and those Islands; and that being discouraged by the improbability of their ever regaining their native country, and destitute of all their accustomed means of improvement, they have descended, in the course of ages, into their present state of barbarism. None can object to this theory, on account of the diversity of features, complexion, and languages, who hold that the human race have descended from one common parentage; since, time and circumstances may have wrought a chanage in this case, as well as in that. The circumstances which lead us to this opinion are these: about fifty years ago, as we were informed, by different gentlemen, connected with the Hudson's Bay Fur Company, and previous to their establishment in that country, a Japanese Junk was cast upon the North West coast of Oregon; the people who saved themselves from the wreck were taken, and enslaved by the Indians, and were found among them, by the Company's Traders, in that condition. They endeavored to purchase them from their masters, but were unable to obtain them at any reasonable price. The Company, after the expiration of several years, found it necessary to employ a steamer, to collect their furs, on this coast; and instructed the master, upon its arrival, to obtain, if possible, the Japanese slaves. The Indians, whose villages were near the Sea shore, were at the time of the

Steamer's arrival on that coast, many of them, out in their canoes, some distance from land. As soon as they perceived her, they fled for the shore, and the steamer persuing, so terrified them, that they not only abandoned their canoes, but their villages also, and fled *en masse*, to the mountains, leaving not only the Japanese, but every thing else behind them. The Japanese were taken on board the steamer, conveyed to Fort Vancouver, and sent from there to London, whence they were carried on board an East Indiaman, to their native country. And beside this, there are the remains of a wreck, near Cape Look Out, at which the Indians have frequently collected beeswax, which was thrown out on the beach, by the surf; and it is the general impression, that this also, was a Japanese or Chinese vessel. The Indians have some strange and mysterious traditions, concerning this wreck; but we were not able to learn any thing definite from them, concerning its character, or the time of its destruction; but it is evidently many years since it was lost. We know of no account of the loss of any such vessel, from any of the Commercial nations of the world, and it is, at least, probable, that this also, was driven from the shores of the Eastern Continent; and if this were the case, here then, are two instances, in which people have been cast upon the Western shores of America, from China or Japan, perhaps from both; two instances, by which, had the Continent been at those times without inhabitants, it would, or might have been peopled. And since the Chinese Empire has been in existence so long, and since they have been, in many respects, so long enlightened, why may not this have happened, thousands as well as fifty or an hundred years ago; and why may it not have happened, before this Continent was inhabited, and they have been the Parents of the present aborigines?

The scenery in Oregon, is varied, romantic, picturesque, and grand. There is certainly nothing to equal it, in North America, East of the Rocky Mountains; and, although much has been said of the beauty and grandeur of the scenery of Switzerland, we doubt if any thing can be there found to equal it; taking into view, the rich, extensive, and flowery plains, surrounded by tall and heavy forests, of ever-green, watered by many large and living streams, flowing sometimes smooth and gentlle, then rapid, and again precipitating, in broad, and heavy sheets, down immense perpendicular Falls. There may be, some where on the earth's whole surface, some spot which can equal in the mighty grandness of its scenery, the mountains, the valleys, and the shores of Oregon ; but if there be, 'tis vast, 'tis beautiful, 'tis grand indeed. Let the beholder, stand upon the green summit of one of the high isolated hills, that rise from the plain in the upper Willammette, and what a prospect! The imagination that has been accustomed only to the level surface, and dull monotony of the Valley of the Mississippi, must be stretched to its utmost to comprehend the mighty picture. The fair Valley of the Willammette, with its hills, and its vales, its forets, and its plains, is spread out before you. To the East, and extending as far as the eye can reach to the North and South, the Cascades, in one lofty, unbroken range, rise mountain upon mountain, and forest over forest, until their highest peaks, wrapped in eternal snow, and white as the unsullied flake in the storm of Winter, stand high and giddy, far above the clouds. At your feet you can see the Willammette, meandering down the wide fertile Valley, and can trace afar, the course of the broad Columbia, winding through its forest-crested hills; and further away to the North, St. Helens shows her towering crater of eternal fire; and further still, the eye is lost in the wide labrynth of dark and clustering heights, in distance indistinct. Away to the South, the peering summits of some lofty chain, are dimly drawn upon the sky. To the West, you hear the distant Ocean's sullen roar, as its waves, with crash tremendous, break upon its rock bound shores. The bright clear blue above is cloudless; all beneath, seems hushed in deep repose ; even the loud Cataract's thunders, wake not so far the circling waves of air ; and save, perchance, the carol of a mountain bird, the breeze sighing to the leaves, and the heavy murmuring of the distant deep, all else is silent, as it was upon the morn, when God created it. Here may the imagination lift the veil which hides the future, and peer into the destinies of this fair land: As it runs over the wide prospect, it peoples it with thousands and thousands of busy inhabitants, sees every plain checkered with fields, and even the steep and rugged Mountain-side, made to yield to the hand of the husbandman; every where, houses, gardens, orchards, and vinyards, scattered in countless multitudes, over hill and valley ; flocks and herds feeding, on every hand ; the broad highways coursing the valley, or winding away over the hills, thronged with a busy concourse, all moving hurriedly to and fro, engaged in the avocations of a civilized life ; sees villages, towns, and cities, with massive walls and glittering spires, which have risen above the mouldered huts of a departed race. It looks forward to the time when, where now the Indian, upon his jaded horse, is winding along the narrow and solitary trail, the powerful locomotive, with its heavy train, will fly along the rattling railway; when, instead of yon frail canoe, the pround steamer will dash along the majestic river; when that Ocean, now idly breaking on its cragged shores, shall be whitened with the sails of Commerce; and when, amid the flags of an hundred nations, its own proud motto and device, resting on folds gemmed with images, whose bright orignals bestud her skies, shall float proudly superior to them all; when, where now, there is little else than a wild wilderness, there shall be all the life—all the populous throng and bustle—all the stately magnificence—all the interests—all the enterprise—all the intelligence—of th e most active, proud, and populous nations of the Old World. Imagination, peering into the far future, beholds enthroned upon an hundred heights, the lordly mansions of the opulent, surrounded with gardens, teeming with fruits and flowers; with parks, and pools, and groves of ornamental trees; and far up the sides of the surrounding mountains, the herdsmen's and the shepherd's humble cottages repose, in sweet and solitary quiet, deep buried amid the mountain pines. And still, yielding to a more romantic mood, the imagination, excited by every thing about it, and by its own wild pictures, cannot but come, in its dreamy wanderings, to the time when these mountains—these rivers—these verdant vales,—when every rock, and hill, and cataract; when every forest, glade, and glen; when every mountain gorge, and precipice, and dark ravine, shall have been sung and storied, until they have grown old and honored by the Poet's pen, and the thrilling legends of the past. But, looking beyond the snow capped barrier, which bounds the vission, to the East, the mind labors in vain to read, from the character of such dreary regions, what will be the future destiny of those wilds and wastes. Long may the lover of romantic scenes and adventures, find in them an ample scope for all his inclinations. Long may the Poet and writer of fiction, undetected, rear there, the fabricks of their dreams, and people the green mountain-girt Oasis of those unexplored solitudes, with the gallant, lovely, and happy creatures of their imaginations. About these, hang mysteries, which time and the baseless stories of the fanciful, will probably render only more mysterious. In these, may rest at last, the remnant of the ancient owners of this great Continent; and here, in a semi-civilized condition, they may continue, the wonder and the terror of ages yet to be. In such a land as this, it is easy to suppose that the minds of its future inhabitants, partaking of the characters of the things around them, will rise in splendor, like their own cloud-piercing peaks; or flow, in majesty, like their broad, majestic Rivers.

And while beholding here, a prospect, which he feels that nature herself, in her farthest reachings, in her most sublime imaginings, could not improve; to which, though she would scatter with unsparing hand, upon one favored spot, all beauty and all grandeur, she could not add one single touch; while taking, at one vast sweep, such an assemblage of grand various and scenery; and while indulging such fanciful images of the future, the traveler, reclining, perhaps, upon the green sward which clothes the rounded height, from its base to its brow; and beneath the green arms of a low and spreading oak, might revert, amid such silence, and such scenes, to the far land of his home, and recall to his mind others, though less grand and beautiful, yet even dearer than these; might yield to a feeling of regret, when hearing here, the loud Ocean's voice, and seeing yonder, the stern mountain barrier, mingling its snows with cloud and sky; both separating him from that home, and from those cherished scenes.

But to conclude this portion of our subject, by summing up, in short, the advantages and disadvantages, which the Territory of Oregon possesses, in comparison with other countries, or rather, with portions of the United States. We suppose its principal advantages, for instance, over the Valley of the Mississippi, to be, in climate, in its situation for Commerce, in its water power, in its forest of gigantic trees, in the purity of its waters, and in the vastness and beauty of its scenery. In all of these, it is certainly superior.—In respect to its climate, the rainy seasons, it is true, are often disagreeable; but its being favorable to grazing, and most especially, its great healthfulness, renders it very far superior to that of any portion of the States. Its situation for profitable Commerce with other portions of the world, we consider, to be superior also, to that of the Valley of the Mississippi. The vast extent of Sea-coast, embracing every clime; and the numerous fertile Islands, with which the great Pacific Ocean is crowded, to which it has immediate access, render it superior. And the circumstance, that almost all the commercial and manufacturing nations of the world, are compelled to make great circuits, in order to reach these shores, gives another advantage worthy of consideration. Its water power, we believe, cannot be surpassed on the face of the globe; neither can its forests, or the purity of its streams. Its principal disadvantages, (excepting that of the Winter rains,) are the limited extent of the habitable portion, the great amount of waste land; included even in that portion; the different parts of it, which are suitable for settlements, being detached, by ranges of mountains, making access from one to another, often difficult; the rock-bound character of its coast; the inferiority of its inland navigation; and of the soil of the high lands. In all of these, it is surely inferior to the Mississppi Valley. But after balancing the advantages and disadvantages, we cannot determine which is, in reality, superior. Different men have different opinions. One will prefer one country, and another will prefer another country; one will chose the fertile Valley of the Mississippi; another the healthful climate, and the romantic scenery of Oregon.

CHAPTER IV.

ROUTE FROM OREGON TO CALIFORNIA.

Rendezvous—Indian War Dance—Indians came into Camp to trade—Adventure of an Iroquois Indian—An Alarm—SugarPine—Soda Spring—Sacramento River—Sacramento Hills—Rugged Road—Indians on the Sacramento—Fort, Trading Post, &c., of Captain Sutter.

We left the rendezvous near the Methodist Mission, on the Upper Willammette, on the 18th day of June, 1844, for Upper California. Our Company consisted of thirty-seven persons; of which number, thirteen were women and children; the rest were made up of Americans, English, French, Mexicans, and Indians of four different tribes. We took our baggage, entirely with pack animals, as the route will admit of being traveled in no other way.— Proceeding up the Willammette River ninety miles, near to the point where it comes out of the mountains, we left it, and bearing off across the Valley, at ten miles, came to the Calapooiah Mountains; and passed over them, a distance of twelve miles, with ease, into the Valley of the Umqua. Passing across it by a very circuitous way, which characterizes the whole route to California, we came, at sixty miles, to the foot of the Umqua Mountains, and encamped by a small, clear mountain stream, which ran hurriedly along, through a beautiful and extensive inclination, thickly set with a fine green sward; and over which, here and there, the dark green Pines arose to the height of two hundred feet.

Late in the evening, about twenty of the Umqua Indians, came into our Camp. At night, several of them, being induced by a half breed Frenchman, of our party, who was always fond of witnessing and participating in all the games and amusements of his savage brethren, performed one of their War Dances. After equipping and painting themselves, in the most hedious manner which their imaginations, almost perfect in such savage arts, could possibly invent: Having their bows and arrows in their hands, with all their implements of war about them; and being arranged in a row, on one side of the Camp fires; while we, who were looking on, occupied the other; they began dancing; singing, at the same time, in the wildest and most fiend-like strain; making the most hedious grimaces, and every variety of threatening gesture: sometimes throwing into their countenances a most intense gaze, and with lowering brows, and eyes directed along their arrows, as if riveted upon some fated object, upon which they were about to spring, and transfix with a deadly weapon; they would suddenly bend their bows to the very arrow's head, as if in the act of shooting a foe; then, recovering, with a dreadful smile of savage satisfaction, they would flourish their arms about their heads, and throw into their song a tone of fiendish triumph, such as would compel the stoutest nerves to cringe. During the dance, one of the number, who appeared to act the Chief, and to be bound to excel in the terrible, crouched to one half his natural stature, facing the rest, and if possible more hediously arrayed, kept moving by a short, quick, patting step, from one end of the line to the other. At intervals, when they appeared to have finished one part, they would all straighten themselves up, to their full height, and utter several loud, shrill, piercing yells, which thrilled through the forest, and was echoed back from every tree, and the distant hills, as if a host had answered; then again, they would commence the dancing and singing, as before, varying it with the same wild grimaces and gestures, and again conclude with the same loud, thrilling yells; until, after performing in this manner, several times, they wound up by a sham attack. This they did, by holding the bow in their left hand, and grasping the arrow on the string with the right, (as is usual with them;) resting the right hand on the hip; drawing the bow with all their strength; throwing themselves forward and back, and bending their bodies, until their heads almost touched the ground; and all the time they were springing about, in every direction, as if avoiding the missiles of the foe, and yelling at the very top of their voices, with more than mortal fierceness. During this performance of the Indians, the Camp fires burning bright, lighted up the surrounding forest to a considerable distance, showing the tall green pines, and leaving all beyond, (though the moon was high,) in deep dense darkness; giving to the wild scene so wildly acted, in those far savage solitudes, additional wildness; so far surpassing what we commonly consider to belong to nature and reality, that one seemed to dream; and standing in Tartarian shades, to gaze upon the regions of the damned.

In the morning, we commenced the ascent of the Umqua Mountains, which, being covered with thick timber and brush, was considered as a place favorable to the Indians for an attack; and as we were approaching the territory of the hostile Rascals, (a tribe of Indians frequently so called,) who previously never allowed a favorable opportunity for an attack to pass unimproved, there was much uneasiness in camp, and preparations were made to prevent a surprise. Front, flank, and rear guards were kept out, while the party were moving, and some of the *braves* put on their defensive armor, in the shape of extra shirts, pants, vests, coats, and over coats, to ward off the arrows of the ambushed Rascals. We, however, passed over the mountain, a distance of fourteen miles, without seeing or hearing from the Indians, and came into the Valley of Rogue's River. At the crossing of the River, thirty of the Rascals came into camp, for the purpose of opening a trade. They were, at first, very shy in approaching us. When within two hundred yards, they halted; and waited some time. regarding us closely, in order to ascertain, from our movements, whether we were disposed to be friends or foes. After repeatedly assuring them of our friendship, and persuading them a long time, they at length came very slowly and cautiously within twenty yards of us, and took their seats in a row, on the ground. In all their movements, and in every expression of their countenances, nothing could be detected that indicated fear, although it was certain, that they were far from being destitute of such sensations; they held such complete command over their nerves, and knew so well how to dissemble that all appeared to be nothing more than caution. Having prepared a pipe and tobacco, several of our party arranged themselves in a circle with the Indians, and smoked, passing the pipe around to the left, from one to another. This is a mark of friendship, and amounts to a treaty of peace. After smoking and asking our permission to depart, which is a custom among the Indians, in the place of our "Good night," they retired, promising to return. In the morning, they came again to our encampment, bringing with them quite a number of beaver skins; which they exchanged with different individuals of our company, for such trifling articles as they pleased to give them.

Having passed across the Valley of Rogue's River, a distance of fifty miles, we came to the Chesty Mountains. Here, the trail, taking a narrow spur of the Mountain, on either side of which, there was a small ravine full of think brush, gave the Indians a favorable opportunity for making an attack; and, as we knew of their having before attacked Companies at this place, and doing considerable damage; here again, we used the previous precaution, of putting out the necessary guards; and the *braves* again put on their armour, and again we passed in safety the dangerous mountain, and crossed over into the valley beyond, a distance of only six miles, without encountering any difficulty. Having crossed the Northern side of the Valley, and also the Clamuth River, we encamped early in the evening, at a small spring, three miles beyond the River, and thirteen from the foot of the Chesty Mountains. Here an Iroquois Indian of our Company, having returned from a hunting excursion, reported that, while hunting, he came suddenly upon a small Indian camp; and being perceived by the Indians, he went boldly in, as if his coming had been intentional. This scheme, of course, gave the Indians to believe that he considered, from some cause, perhaps the vicinity of a strong party, that he had no reason to be afraid. It worked well, and he returned without being molested, having noticed, as he said, several horses in the Indian camp.—Upon hearing this last part of the story, three of our party, an American, a Frenchman, and a half breed, named Petitoo, set out, against the protest of the whole camp, declaring that they would have the horses. Night came on, and all had retired to bed, when the Indian yell was raised within a few hundred yards; and every one supposing that the party had been killed by the Indians, and that they were coming upon the camp, sprang to their arms, and hastened to meet what they supposed to be an enemy. It proved, however, to be the three themselves, who in their wild and unwarrantable glee, breaking over all custom, and acknowledged laws of order and propriety, wished, for mere sport, to put the camp in a panic. They came charging up at full speed, and Petitoo, who was the ring-leader in the affair, to make a sort of "grand flourish," put whip and spur to his jaded horse, already scarcely able to proceed and coming into the staking ground at a rapid rate, was about to rein up before the crowd, who had rushed out to meet "the Indians," and was just crying out, with a swaggering air, "*Caraho pindaho!*" a favorite Spanish exclamation, when his horse, tangled in one of the staking ropes, fell; and, turning a complete somerset, went tumbling after his rider, who was hastening, in spite of himself, by several successive and astonishing feats of "grand and lofty tumbling," to the bottom of the hill, amid the peals of laughter and cursings, that burst from the still half-terrified camp. After having received a severe reprimand, and a promise of something severer if they ever dared to alarm the Company again, the frolicking party sneaked off to bed, crest-fallen and disappointed.

Continuing across the Clamuth Valley, which is nearly destitute of timber, we came, at thirty miles, to its Southern side, which is a low division, between the waters of the Clamuth and the Sacramento, and is covered with a forest of Pine and Fir. There we saw the first of the Sugar Pine, one of the largest and finest of the Pine species: it is frequently found ten feet in diameter, and two hundred and fifty feet high. The wood of this species is probably superior to the best common Pine. It is called Sugar Pine, from the peculiar quality of its gum, which tastes very much like Sugar saturated with Turpentine. A small portion of this gum operates as a mild and efficient purgative. Here, on our right, is a high range of Mountains extending North and South; and on our left, the Snowy Butte, a lofty isolated peak, rises from the bosom of an extensive plain, far into the region of eternal snow, and gives rise to the West branch of the Secramento River, which we struck in ten miles after leaving the Clamuth Valley, and continued down it, frequently crossing and recrossing the stream. Fifteen miles below the point where we first struck this stream, we came to a Soda spring, bursting out from the foot of a high hill, and running into a small basin, formed by travelers or Indians, for the convenience of drinking. The water of this Spring is strongly impregnated with some other mineral. From this Soda Spring, we proceeded down the River, through the Sacramento Hills, which are high, steep, and rugged; covered with timber, and almost destitute of grass. The rock in these hills is principally a coarse granite; but that forming the channel of the River is volcanic. In passing through these hills we were still compelled to cross and recross the stream, in order to find a passable way, which, in its whole course, until it reaches the head of the Valley, a distance of one hundred miles, is full of falls, rapids, and narrow canions. Having come to the head of the Valley, we took the west side of the River, which here begins to assume a different character, losing its irregularity and rapidity, and flowing with a more even current. Continuing down the Valley, on the West side, we found, all along on the River, villáges of Indians, living in miserable huts made of poles, set on end in a circle on the ground, leaned together, fastened at the top, and covered with grass and dirt. We found those in the upper part of the Valley, entirely naked; and so wild, that they fled from our approach, into the thickets, leaving their villages and all their property behind them. They subsist, principally, upon salmon, (which ascend the River in great quantities,) upon acorns, and wild oats.

One hundred and sixty miles from the head of the valley, we came to the Fort of Capt. Sutter, a large trading establishment, built of dobies. Capt. Sutter's Fort is situated on the East side of the Sacramento River, about fifty miles above its entrance into the Bay of St. Francisco, at the head of tide water, and some distance below the affluance of the Rio de los Americanos, or the Ameircan River, a stream which has its source in the Mountains to the East. It is in latitude 38 deg. 35 min. North, and is the principal place in the Sacramento Valley, and one to which the foreigners who are residing in Upper California, look for refuge and protection, in case of an out break by the Indians, or an attempt on the part of the Spaniards, to expel them from the country. The Fort is a quadrangular wall, built of large sun-dried brick, and has bastions in the corners, in which are mounted several small pieces of artillery. It is garrisoned by about forty Indians; one of whom, constantly stands sentry, during the day, as well as the night, and apprises those in the Fort, of the approach of any party, whether friends or foes. It covers a large area, and is probably capable of containing a garrison of one thousand men. Within the walls, are the shops, and the residences of the officers, mechanics, and servants; and there is, also, connected with the establishment, a horse mill, a distillery, and a tannery. Captain Sutter, at first, had difficulties with the Indians; but by the promptness, and severity with which he has frequently chastised them; whether he acted against tribes, or individuals, against Chiefs or subjects; has at length brought them to fear, and respect him; and now they seldom molest his property or the men in his employ. The Indians cultivate, and improve his farms, attend to his large herds of animals, make a portion of his trapping parties, and do all the drudgery about the Fort: hundreds of them are ready, also, to defend him against any emergency. The government of California was, at first, suspicious of him, on account of the strength of his fortifications, and the influence which he was acquiring over the Indians; but he has since been appointed an officer of Justice by them. It is, however, very doubtful, whether their former feelings towards him, are changed: were it not for the insufficiency of their power, it is believed, that they would yet banish him from the country. Capt.

Sutter is a native of Switzerland, and came from Missouri to his present location, and has been in California about five years: he purchased the cannon and other portions of the establishment, of a Russian Company, then in the country; and having obtained, of the Mexican Government, a grant of land along the Sacramento River, of some thirty or forty square leagues; he removed to his present situation. Besides the fur trade, he carries on an extensive business in farming, stock raising, and manufacturing. He has a very large farm, and large bands of cattle, horses, sheep, and hogs, and constantly keeps employed, mechanics of different descriptions.—He is spoken of, by all who visit him, as being very accommodating, hospitable, and altogether, much of a gentleman; nor have we any disposition, to differ with the general impression. Here our company disbanded; some going to one, and some to another part of the province.

CHAPTER V.

DESCRIPTION OF UPPER CALIFORNIA.

Bay of Francisco—Sacramento and St. Wakine Valleys—Many narrow fertile Valleys—Great Lake, &c.—Barren Mountains, containing Silver Ore and good Water Power—Tar Spring—Gold found in the Puebalo Valley—Cultivation of the Vine—Spanish Dance—Wild Horses—Unsuccessful attempt to take them.

That portion of Mexican Territory, which is generally alluded to under the of name California, is included between the Pacific coast, and the California Mountains; a lofty and rugged range, which is a continuation of the Cascade Mountains, in Oregon, running nearly parallel with the coast, and East of it about one hundred and twenty-five miles; and between the parallel of 42 deg. North, and the Gulf of California. But the Southern part of this district, including the Peninsula, called Lower California, is a poor, dry, barren region, and has not yet afforded inducements sufficient to attract the attention of foreigners. That portion which is most desirable, and to which persons from the United States, traveling through, and settling in the country, have entirely confined their attention, is called Upper California; and is that part lying between the head of the Gulf, and the Northern boundary of the Province: and to this portion, we shall be confined in our remarks.

The Bay of San Francisco, situated in latitude 37° 45′ North, is, perhaps, without exception, the finest and most spacious Harbor on the globe. It has been spoken of, and we believe without exaggeration, as being of sufficient capacity to contain all the Shipping of the world. The entrance of the Bay, is only about one mile wide. It increases rapidly in width, after entering the land; and separating, forms two arms; one bearing to the South East, the other to the North East. The Southern arm, is fifty miles in length, and ten in width, and is a beautiful sheet of water; deep, and entirely free from sand-banks and Islands. The Northern arm, is sixty miles in length, and about ten in width; is very crooked, containing many small islands; and has numerous creeks and coves, every where indenting its shores. The St. Wakine and Sacramento Rivers, empty at the head of this arm of the Bay; the former from the South East, and the latter from the North. They are both streams susceptible of navigation, and their valleys uniting, form the most extensive body of level land, found any where on the Western coast; being from the head of one valley to that of the other, about four hundred miles in length: and in width, from the California Mountains West, about fifty miles. There are numerous small streams running through these valleys, from the mountains, and from the highlands on the West, into the rivers; on all of which, there are rich and productive strips of land, from three to four miles in width, and extending back to the mountains. There are generally, along these streams, narrow belts of Oak timber, of which there are three kinds: White, Black, and an inferior kind of Live Oak. The trunks are short, and none are well calculated for fencing. Between the streams, the land is less fertile, very dry, and not at all adapted to cultivation; it, nevertheless, produces an abundance of the richest kind of grass, capable of affording support, during the whole year, to large herds of cattle and horses.

On the California Mountains, and on many of the inclinations, between them and the valleys, there is a timber called Red Wood; a large and very fine tree, of the Pine species, peculiar to California; Cedar and Sugar Pine, in inexhaustible abundance. But that part is generally considered, the best portion of the Province, which lays West of the Sacramento Valley, and North of the Bay of San Francisco. It consists of alternate hills and valleys.—Many of the hills are high; but they are gradual and unbroken.—The valleys are from three to four miles in width, and from fifty to sixty in length; are all traversed by small streams of water, and have an excellent soil. Those which connect with the Bay—of which there are five or six—run from North to South. Those which connect with the coast, and with the valley of the Sacramento, run to the West, and East. Immediately on the coast North of the Bay, there is a range of very high, rolling hills, which increase in height to the North. They are covered with oats, which is a sponatneous production of this country; with excellent grass, and with groves and forests of Red Wood and Oak.

One hundred miles North of the Bay, and at about an equal distance from the Sacramento Valley and the coast, is the Great Lake, which is, in length from North to South, sixty miles, and fifteen in width. It is said to be a beautiful, clear sheet of water, surrounded by a belt of fine alluvial prairie, which also, is encircled by a wall of high Mountains, covered in many places, with groves of Red Wood and Oak, and giving rise to numerous rivulets, which meander across the plain, and empty into the Lake.—This is perhaps, the most beautiful, romantic, and picturesque portion of the Province; but its very secluded situation, having, as far as has yet been learned, no good natural communication with the surrounding country, renders it less valuable. North of the Great Lake, the country is, as far as the Clamuth Valley, little else than a vast cluster of mountains; which, connected by the Sacramento Hills, join with the spurs of the California Mountains, and form the Northern boundary to the habitable portion of the Province.

The Southern arm of the Bay of San Francisco, is surrounded by a belt of level land; which, on the North side, is six or eight miles in width, and very fertile. Francisco or Yerba Buena is a small town, situated on the point of land South of the entrance of the Bay, and has a popualtion of about two hundred.—The land upon which it is built, rises gradually one mile from the Bay, and descends gradually the same distance, to the Ocean; and its situation, for a commercial town, is generally considered to be the best, and most advantageous, in California.

The country South of the Bay, and between the St. Wakine and the coast, is also diversified with mountains and valleys. The mountains are high and some of them are barren. The valleys are fertile, from three to four miles wide, and from forty to fifty long. Their course is from South East to North West; and the streams, by which they are watered, empty into the Bay. Further South, the streams rising in the California Mountains, South of the head of the St. Wakine, run West, and empty into the Ocean. They have rich valleys four and five miles in width, covered with grass and clover, and separted by high mountains; some of which are covered with forests of Red Wood and scattering Oaks, and others are barren. Among the barren mountains, in many places silver is found in abundance; but little or no attention has ever been paid to it, and none of the mines have yet been worked. The

Ore is said to be of good quality, and easily obtained. This part of the territory is well watered, and affords some good sites for machinery.

Monte Rey, the Capitol of the Province, is situated at the termination of one of these valleys, near the mouth of a small river, and on the bay of Monte Rey, an inlet affording a harbor for shipping, but too much exposed to the Sea, to be a good and safe one. The town is small, containing only a population of about three hundred persons; and is built principally of dobies. Forty miles North East from Monte Rey, there is a bituminous, or Tar Spring, oozing out from the foot of a mountain, and covering several acres of ground. This bitumen or mineral Tar, is said to answer well, all the purposes for which common Tar is used: it is inflammable, and becomes hard by exposure to the atmosphere.

South from Monte Rey, for several hundred miles, there are no valleys of considerable size, or country fit for cultivation; being a succession of high mountains, as far as Santa Barbara. Timber is scarce in this mountainous district, but it is, nevertheless, considered valuable for grazing; being covered with an abundance of oats, and various kinds of nutricious grass. At Santa Barbara, there is a fine valley, about five miles in width, and sixty in length. Immediately South of this valley, and separated from it by a mountain, is the lower Pueblo Valley, of about the same size. These valleys have a black alluvial soil, and are both traversed by small rivers, rising in the mountains to the East, flowing to the West, and emptying into the Ocean. They have numerous small tributaries, which arise in the bordering mountains, and empty from either side.

The great objection to this portion of the country is that it is almost entirely destitute af timber. Gold is found in considerable quantities, in the upper part of the Pueblo Valley; yet the inconvenience of water, renders the working of the mines less profitable. A company was formed, however, about the time of our leaving the country, to engage in this business. The Pueblo, and Santa Barbara, are both towns of considerable size; containing each, probably, a population of about two thousand. They are situated about twenty miles from the sea shore, and the inhabitants are engaged in stock raising, and the cultivation of the vine. There is anchorage for shipping, at the Western termination of these valleys.

The Southern portion of the Province of California, called Lower California, is more populous than the portion which we have been considering; but its population consists almost entirely of Mexican Spaniards, and Indians; there being but very few "Foreigners" in that part of California. (The term Foreigners, is used here to designate all others, except the Mexican Spaniards, and Indians; though they have been residents in the country for many years; have become citizens; or even though they have been born in the country; still they are foreigners, if they be the descendants of Americans, English, French, Dutch, or of any other people, except those whom we have excepted.) We have never traveled through Lower California, and are, therefore, incapable of making statements concerning it. But we have been informed, by those who were acquainted with it, that a great portion of it is mountainous, dry, and sterile; and especially the Peninsula of California: and, although we have never tested, by actual observation, the correctness of this description, yet we have some corroborating evidence of its truth; since we have observed, in proceeding South, from the Bay of San Francisco, that the country becomes, as we advance, gradually less fertile, and less favorable to vegetation; the cultivated land, requiring frequent arrigation, to counteract the effect of the Summer droughts: we have also observed that the country becomes more mountainous; the valleys less productive; and that timber, is often, almost entirely wanting. From this, we would conclude, and we think, not without a good degree of reason, that in advancing still farther to the South, we would, probably, find the country agreeing with the description, which our informants have given. The fact, that there are so few foreigners in that portion of the country, leads to the opinion that there is little inducement for them to settle there. Were it otherwise, we might be sure of finding Americans, at least; for there is no country, of considerable extent, upon the earth's surface, which offers either pleasure or profit, where some of our adventurous countrymen, are not to be found, unless their entrance is prohibited by the laws, or prevented by opposing arms.

Between the Northern and the Southern arms of the Bay of San Francisco, there is a range of high lands commencing, which, after running a short distance in a South East course, trends away to the South, until their general course is about parallel with the coast. They separate the waters of the Southern arm of the Bay of San Francisco, and those of the Bay of Monte Rey, (the Rio San Buenevantura,) from the St. Wakine or Rio San Joaquin, which as we have said, empties into the Northern arm. Trending again to the East, they probably intersect with the California Mountains, South of the head of the San Joaquin, bounding its valley on the West and South, and giving rise, on one side, to the tributaries which come into it, from those directions, and on the other, to the Eastern tributaries of the Rio San Buenevantara, and to some other smaller streams, which rise South of this, and empty into the Ocean.

The soil of the Valley of the St. Wakine, along the river, and on its tributaries, is very rich, and consequently, favorable to agricultural productions. These fertile strips, make up a great portion of the valley; but beside these, there are extensive tracts of barren land, laying back, between the river and the mountains, and between its tributaries. These barren tracts, are so dry and sandy, as to be entirely unfit for cultivation; but they are, nevertheless, covered with that superior kind of grass, peculiar to these Western countries; and which, although it is much less abundant on the barren, than on the fertile land, is richer and more nutritious. On this account, these unfruitful lands, are not altogether valueless; affording, as they do, excellent pasturage for large herds of cattle. In one portion of this valley, the land is so sandy, that several of the mountain streams, which would otherwise empty into the River, are swallowed up. This portion is of considerable extent, and the river, for a long distance opposite to it, receives no tributaries, from that side.

It will seem contradictory, that lands unfit for cultivation, and so dry, as we have represented these to be, should produce grass sufficient to render them valuable, for the purpose of grazing: but, it must be remembered, that during the rainy season, the frequent showers keep, even these, almost constantly moist; and that the temperature, at this season, is of sufficient mildness, to favor vegetation; and the fact of the grass becoming cured during the dry season, causes them to afford nourishment for animals, constantly. It is improbable, that they will bear pasturage to the same extent, or support the same number of animals, as the fertile lands. But when the country becomes well populated, and when all the lands, adapted to cultivation, shall have been brought into requisition, for that purpose; then these barren lands, with proper care, will give support, the most healthy and nutritious, to immense numbers of all kinds of herbiverous animals.

This, however, is not to be considered, as the general character of the Valley of the St. Wakine; on the contrary, it is considered to be one of the best portions of California. In many places, where the tributaries of the St. Wakine enter the Valley, there are the terminations of narrow, but rich, and beautiful valleys; which wind away among unexplored, and rugged spurs and peaks, and penetrate deep into the bosom of the California Mountains.

In the upper extremity of the Valley of the St. Wakine, there are large lakes, or marshes, called *tulares*, from the *tulé*, (bull rushes.) with which they are filled. It grows to an astonishing size, and so thick, that it is almost impossible to pass through it. This tulé when it falls, covers the marshes, in places, to the depth of more than two feet. There is one of the tulares here, in particular, which is very large, has several streams emptying into it, and covers an extent of many miles. There are others, similar to these, in different parts of the country; there is said to be a large one, through which the River, which empties into the Southern arm of the Bay of San Francisco, flows; and there are some, in the Valley of the Sacramento. There has yet been made, no permanent settlement, in the Valley of St. Wakine. The causes of this, are, that until now, there were other portions of the country, which were thought to offer greater inducements to the settler; and the Indians, who live in the bordering mountains, and who roam through the valley, are, by no means to be trusted. In consequence of there having been no settlements made here, the Valley of the St. Wakine, abounds with all kinds of game, common to the country. Elk, in large bands, are scattered over it, in every direction. Deer are numerous. And there are Antelopes and Bears, also. The tulares, and the streams, are crowded with deafning swarms of waterfowls. All of these different kinds of game, at certain seasons, get to be very fat. There are other wild animals in the St. Wakine Valley. There are many wolves; and wild horses, in bands of many hundreds, may be seen at all times, feeding on its extensive prairies.

At the source of one of the Upper and Eastern tributaries of the St. Wakine, is Walker's Pass; through which, Captain Walker, the discoverer of the Pass, conducted, in the Autumn of 1843, a part of the California emigrants, with whom we traveled from the States to Fort Hall. More frequently it is called "the Point of the Mountain." It is described, as being a beautiful, though narrow, valley, cutting the mountain from its summit almost to its base; affording the only good, natural pass, through this rugged, barrier into the valuable portion of California.— Through this, with a little labor, it is believed, that a very passable wagon road may be made: but being near the parallel of 35 deg., it is entirely too far to the South, to be of much advantage to emigrants from the United States, who cross the Rocky Mountains, at the Great Pass. This Pass, through the Rocky Mountains is in latitude 42 deg. 23 min., and the point on the Pacific coast, where Emigrants would wish, generally, to terminate their journey, is between the latitudes 37 and 38 deg.; so that, after striking the California Mountains, they would have to make, nearly five degrees of Southing—out of their course—in order to pass around "the Point of the Mountains;" and afterwards, to make nearly three of Northing to regain what they had lost. This would be making a circuit, of between four and five hundred miles, in order to accomplish, that, which, by a different route, might be accomplished in about two hundred. This shorter route is, however, a very steep, rugged, and difficult one; but preferable, we believe, to the other, on account of the great difference in distance. But should emigrants go into California, by the way of Taos; or by some more Southern Pass through the Rocky Monntains, than that by which they go at the present; then will Captain Walker's Pass, be found an excellent way, into the Western portion of this country. It will, also, be of the utmost importance, to emigrants, who may be overtaken, by the rainy season; as it is seldom, if ever, obstructed by the snows, which immediately after the commencement of the rains, cover all the mountains; blocking up every other way, to such a dregree, that it is extremely hazardous to attempt them.

This little Valley of verdure and flowers, looks out, from its Eastern extremity, upon an arid desert, over which, in the vast scope which the eye embraces, nothing presents, save huge piles and masses of dark rock, and thirsty sands. In this region, so wonderful, and so unlike any other portion of the known world, even the foot prints of the bold trapper, have seldom disturbed the inhospitable sands. There are a few tracks in the vast region which lies between the California and Rocky Mountains, traveled at times, by the Trappers, and by the Mexican Traders; but these are rare: between them, are extensive spaces, which have never been trodden, by the foot of civilized man. Previously, this has been marked, on the otherwise very imperfect, and incorrect maps, which have been made of the countries West of the Rocky Mountains, "the unexplored region." It was left a perfect blank; and it is strange, that in this very acknowwldgment of their ignorance the map-makers have described, so acurately, what succeeding explorations have proved, to be a perfect blank. It is reasonable to suppose, that the All-Wise, has arranged every thing in nature, with perfect fitness; that there is nothing, in the great globe, which is not perfectly adapted to some proper purpose; which is not a necessary part, in this vast, harmonious machine—the Universe of God. But, as far as the eye of man, though aided by all his philosophy, has yet been able to see; the half of all is unaccountable. So is this seeming waste. It appears to have been thrown in, merely to fill up space; or, to be a barrier, to the commerce, and intercourse of man. To us, a great portion of it, is more than a blank; we would rather have buried, not only a part, but the whole of it, beneath the billows of a vast inland sea. In other respects, the map-makers have been less correct; ignorant that these arid sands could swallow up all the rivers, and torrents, and melted snows of the surrounding mountains, they omitted the loftiest range in North America, in order that the waters of Lake Timpanagos, (the Great Salt Lake,) might flow into the Bay of San Francisco. That was useless. They are thirsty still: the Rio Colerado, were it not protected by a wall of Mountains, would never reach the Gulf of California. There are many lakes besides this, and many streams, running down from the mountains, which enclose this Valley of the Great Salt Lake; all of which, are swallowed up in the sands. The Valley of the Salt Lake, has no outlet. The lofty range, which separates it from the Pacific, has yielded only to the Columbia. The Cascade Mountains, have been severed, only by the great River of the West; and the California Mountains, (an extension of the same,) are unbroken. They stand, like a mighty wall, to separate the green valleys of Western California, from this parched waste.

This Eastern portion of California, however, like Eastern Oregon, contains some green spots, to show more effectually, the dreariness of all around them. Along the Eastern base of the California Mountains, there are, probably, enough of these productive spots, to induce men, in time, to inhabit them. They might be made somewhat profitable, for grazing. There is a region, of considerable extent, in the neighborhood of the Great Salt Lake, which would afford excellent pasturage. There are also, on some of the streams which empty into it, narrow valleys, which have a good soil. Only a portion of this, however, was seen by ourselves; our knowledge concerning it depends, partially, upon the information of others; together with our knowldge, of the general character of the country. A great portion of this habitable region, lies North of the forty second parallel of North latitude, and is, consequently, in the Oregon Territory.

But there is a large portion of the desert region, of which there is little or nothing known. What is known, concerning it, has been learned by merely passing through it, in a few places, by routes, seprated from each other, by great interveing distances; yet from the dreariness of every track, that has yet been tried, may be infered with a good degree of certainty, what those portions are, which have ye. either repelled the efforts of the traveler, the trader, and the trapper; or deterred them, by their very appearance, from attempting to break in upon the secrecy of their gloomy and forbiding solitudes.

With a very few exceptions, in this whole vast scope of territory, lying immediately beyond the Rocky Mountains, extending West several hundred miles, and to an uncertain distance North and South, there can never locate any civilzed society. Their inhabitants will be like those in the Deserts of Arabia, and in the Sahara of Africa.

The climate of California, like that of Oregon, is much milder than in the same latitudes, any where East of the Rocky Mountains. In fact, it is in every respect, very similar to the climate of Oregon; excepting only, that it is warmer in proportion to its difference of latitude, and is dryer: there being not so much rain, during the winter season, and scarcely any during the summer. It is very mild; ice seldom ever being seen in the valleys, or snow, except upon the mountains. The extremes of heat and cold, are not great; nor is the climate sebject to any great and sudden changes. The atmosphere is so pure, that whole beeves will remain sweet and good, in the open air without salt, at any season of the year, for three or four days at a time. The nights are quite cool, during the whole year; and sickness of any kind, is scarcely known or thought of. Nearly all the products of temperate climates, except Indian Corn, flourish here. Oats and clover grow spontaneously, in almost every part of the Province. The vine flourishes as well, perhaps, in California, as in any other portion of the world; and its fruit is the finest, and decidedly the most delicious, that we have ever tasted. There are many large vinyards in different parts of the country, from which several thousand barrels of wine are annually made. Many of the tropical fruits come to perfection here. The prickly pear is cultivated for its fruit. The peach and pear do well; but the apple is not so fine as in the United States. In the Southern part of California, irrigation is necessary, to the production of wheat and garden vegetables; but in the North, this is seldom the case; the late winter rains being sufficient to perfect the harvest. But a small portion of the Province is yet in cultivation; the Spaniards, who comprise the chief population, being engaged principally, in rearing and herding cattle and horses; for which, both the climate and country are peculiarly adapted. Many individuals own several thousand animals; which are kept in bands, and require only the attention of a herdsman. They are always very wild, and can be managed only by force. They are driven into a corál, (a strong enclosure,) once every year, for the purpose of branding, &c. The Spaniards enter these coráls on horse back, with the lassoo, which is a rope, made of raw hide, very strong, and formed into a running noose. Holding one end of this rope, coiled in the left hand, they swing the extended noose with the right several times above the head, in order to open it, and to acquire momentum, and then throw it, with almost unerring precision, from thirty to forty feet, about the head of any animal they choose, making fast the end which they retain, around the horn of the saddle, which is made very strong, and bound firmly upon the horse. The horse, as well as the rider, understands the manner of manœuvering, and is able to hold the strongest bullock; taking care to watch closely its movements, when it is disposed to make battle, and avoiding its furious passes, until it becomes exhausted, or assistance is given to the person who has cought the animal.

These Spaniards are probably equal, in horsemanship, to any people in the world, the famous Arabs of the Eastern deserts, and the wild Cumanches of the great Western praries, not excepted. Many of their feats are entirely increditable, to those who are not well acquainted with their character. We have heard it frequently said, (and it is nearly true,) that the Mexican Spaniard does every thing on horseback and with the lassoo. The Californians like most other Mexican Spaniards, are a lazy, indolent and cowardly people, and have neither enterprise nor spirit of improvement in their disposition, they are only a grade above the aborigines, and like them they will soon be compelled from the very nature of things, to yield to the swelling tide of Anglo-Saxon adventure.

Almost every thing which the Californians possess, is of the rudest and simplest construction. Among the better class, however, there are many exceptions to the general rule; but the great majority of the Californians, who are of Spanish descent, will be embraced under it. Their houses, which are constructed of mud and poles, are often, without either floors or chimneys. Within, they are filthy, and destitute of almost all the furniture, most commonly used by civilized people; even chairs, beds, and tables, are wanting. The earthen floor, without any addition, affords them convenient seats, and with the addition of a bullock's hide, it is made to answer the purpose, of both table and bedsteads. Their cooking utensils, and diet, are rough, and simple, as their furniture; even those who are not of the lowest grade, live almost entirely on beef; and after the manner of their brother aborigines, a wooden stake, sharpened at both ends, so as to form a spit, answers the purpose of pot and platter.

The principal business of all classes, is attending to animals; there are some, however, who cultivate small patches of ground. In doing this, they use plows of the most simple and primitive style. Their plows are nothing more than the fork of a tree, so cut and trimmed, that one of the prongs answers as a beam, by which it is drawn, the other prong is the plow itself, and the main stem, with some trimming, makes the handle. The Spaniards do not, however, often engage in laborious exercise. They are generally content with merely living; and in a country possessed of so mild a climate, as California has, it requires very little exertion to live. Where labor must be performed, they usually employ the Indians, who are obtained for a mere nominal compensation. In fact, a great many of the Indians in California, are little else than slaves.

A wheeled carriage is seldom used by a Californian; a horse and rope answers his purpose. Often, when he goes to any of the towns, to purchase an article, he fastens his money—which is a bullock's hide—to one end of his lassoo; and then mounting his horse, winds the other end around the horn of his saddle, and putting spurs, dashes off at a furious rate, over hill and plain, with, or without a road, to the town.

Their saddles, which are made very strong, are loaded with various trappings, have large heavy wooden stirrups, and altogether, frequently weigh sixty or seventy pounds. The plan of the saddle tree, is an excellent one, and the saddles are very safe and pleasant for the rider; and when they are well constructed, with the exception of their weight, are easy on the animal.

It is difficult to find a people, or even an individual, who has not some good trait of character; and even these Californians, with all their faults, are hospitable at their houses. If a stranger goes to one of their houses, he is made welcome to whatever it affords, and as comfortable as their limited means will allow; he must, however, furnish his own bed. It is always expected that a traveler in California will carry that article with him. When he departs, nothing is demanded, and nothing will be received by them, as a compensation; the almost universal and beautiful reply is, when payment is proffered: "No, God will pay."

There are now about five hundred foreigners residing in the country, and the principal portion are from the United States. Emigration from the United States is rapidly increasing, and it is probable that our citizens will possess themselves of this beautiful and healthy country, with its many vales of fertile land. They will soon outnumber the Spaniards, and gain the ascendency over them. The consequence will be, to throw off their present form of government, establish a Republic of their own, and render this portion of our globe, what nature has seemed to design it should be, a prosperous and happy country.

Grants of land are still obtained from the government, of from one to ten leagues. These grants cannot, however, be had at all times, or by all persons; only those who are in favor with the authorities, are likely to get lands.

The duties on foreign imports, are exceedingly high, and all foreign articles, for which there is any demand, bear a great price. Smuggling is common, and presents are said to turn away the eyes of the Government Officers, and lessen their estimates upon the value of cargoes.

The Government is under the direction of a Governor, appointed by the authorities of the Mexican Government, and the officers of justice are the same as in her other Provinces; they are called Alcaldes, are elected by the people, and have powers very similar to our Justices of the Peace; but the influence of bribery and favoritism affects, in a great degree, the principles of justice, and almost entirely defeats the administration of the laws; and its remoteness from the Capital renders the influence and control of the National Government very limited. They have a regularly organized militia and a small standing army, in the country; but the rebellion of last winter drove the army, with the Governor, out of the Province.

The Spaniards of California are very dissipated, and are exceedingly fond of dressing and amusement. This character applies in a greater or less degree to all, but those only of the higher and wealthier class can indulge these dissipations, to much extent. They are unfeeling and cruel, and many of their amusements partake of this character. They love to witness combats between the Wild Bull and Grizly Bear; for this purpose, a strong arena is formed with heavy palisades, and the animals are taken wherever they can be found, with the lassoo, and dragged into the arena. By them, a Bull is taken, and managed without difficulty; but the Bear, with all their skill and horsemanship, is still a powerful opponent: yet, four or five of these Californians, mounted on their strongest horses, will even take this powerful and ferocious animal alive, and convey him several miles, in order to gratify their fondness for barbarous scenes. If a single horseman, unassisted, throws his lassoo about the neck of a Grizly Bear, the Bear seating himself upon his hinder parts, grasps the lassoo in his fore paws, and commences "hauling away," hand over hand, as adroitly as a Jack-Tar; dragging horse and rider together, towards him. In a case of this kind, the only alternative is, to "slip the cable and make sail." But when there are several to assist, they throw their lassoos around the feet of the captured animal, and thus confined, they drag him away. Being placed together in the arena, the two furious animals soon engage with each other, but the Bear, after such rough handling, is so strained, and bruised, and worried, that he is frequently borne down, and gored to death, by his less powerful adversary. They are fond of cock-fighting, also; and horse-racing; and as the Sabbath is both a leisure and lucky day, and one in which they are commanded to do no labor, their sports, generally, come upon that day, and they are attended by all classes, by saint and sinner. But before every thing else, the Californian is passionately fond of his own National dance, the Mexican Fandango. In order to convey some idea of this great favorite Mexican amusement, we will give a brief description of one that went off on a Sunday night, in Sonoma, at the residence of a Spanish gentleman, Don Gaudeloupe Viyeahoes, to attend which, we were favored with an invitation. About candlelighting the guests began to assemble, among whom we were the earliest, in order to witness the whole proceedings. As they arrived, the gentlemen collected in small groups, through the yard, and entered into the discussion of various subjects; and some highly amusing if we might be allowed to judge from appearances, such as teeth shining under black curling mustachoes,—the low chucle, with an occasional loud laugh—while others, with more serious demeanor, were calculating their chances for failure or success, in the pending revolution, for they were rebels, and were consequently interested in the issue. In the meantime, the young ladies, with noisy glee, were frolicking, singing, and dancing within; and some of the married ones were preparing the nicknacks, and getting ready the wines, while others were engaged in arranging and ornamenting the room for the dance. Preparation being ended, we were invited in, and took our seats in a row, on one side of the room, while the ladies, in the same order, occupied the other. The sides of the hall, which was twenty by forty feet, were lined, with persons of every age. The music, which consisted of two guitars and a violin, occupied one end, while the other was filled up by several tables, upon which were heaped indiscriminately, hats, cloaks, coats, and shawls, and the board bearing the sweet breads, wines, &c., which completed the circle, and occupied a large portion of the room. The hall was well lighted, by lamps, suspended from the walls and ceiling; in short, every thing was very well regulated, except only, the disposition of the sexes. A young Don now stepped into the middle of the floor, gave a few shuffles, and the music commenced. He began to pat, or rather to stamp the tune, flat footed: which he continued, without variation, until he had gone through all the different parts of the air. During this time, he had moved to the farther end of the hall, and back again to his starting place; and so exactly had he calculated the measure of his step, that he had occupied precisely the same space of time, in accomplishing his circuit, that was required by the musician, in completing the tune. He then walked up to a young lady, and began clapping his hands in her face, in a manner that reminded us, of a young Hoosier, scaring black birds out of a corn field, or encouraging a lazy cur to take hold of some rascally pig; but we soon learned, that he was only inviting her to dance. So, after clapping his hands half a dozen times, he retired to his seat, and the lady came on to the floor, and went through the same patting and stamping, which the gentleman had done. This mode of dancing had continued for some time, when one of the fair, who was occupying the floor; from fancy, curiosity, or politeness, danced up to an American, and began clapping her hands in his face. Our countryman was evidently very much embarrassed; he blushed, reddened, and at last, after several hems and hawks, stammered out, "*No, sarvy.*" Not at all discouraged at this failure, and resolved, as it seemed, on seeing an American dance; she turned, and went waltzing up to our friend, who by the way, was not easily dashed, though not much of a dancer. "What could I do," said he afterward; "I could not dance in their style, I knew; and but very little in any other: if I took the floor, I might reasonably expect to fail, and so be laughed at, for an awkward American; if I refused, I should be ridiculed for my timidity, and want of gallantry. While thinking thus," said he, "the lady was all the while, with a most persuasive smile, bowing, clapping her hands, and urging her entreaties, with all the English she was acquainted with. I turned my head, saw some of the company beginning to titter, and could bear it no longer." Here he made a desperate effort, gained the middle of the floor, and then went patting away, to the further end of the room; imitating their mode of dancing, as well as he could; then turning, he came down on a real, regular, backwoods hoe-down shuffle; wheeled into the middle of the floor, cut the pigeon wing, and brought up before a pretty brunette, who seemed about to go into a fit of hysterics, from excessive laughter, at the novel performance; clapped his hands four or five times in her face, and then went whirling away to his seat. "Go it countryman—huzzah countryman," cried we, joining in the general uproar. The Spaniards appeared to be much interested, and were quite pleased with this new way of dancing, and during the evening, we saw numbers of both sexes, trying to imitate the step. At length, becoming tired of this single handed game, they changed it, into a series of waltzes, cotilions, &c.; which were performed with such noise and uproar, that we verily believe they might have been heard half a mile. It appeared that skill was estimated, by them, in proportion to the amount of sound produced; which was created in two ways: first, by the heavy dancing, and secondly, by yelling at the top of the voice, parts of the tune, which were designed to chime in with the instruments; but which, however, so far from being the case, when half a dozen of those stentorian voices, at once broke forth, it produced such a variety of horrible discords, as could be compared to nothing, but the simultaneous roar, of a caravan of African and Asiatic animals. At length came the refreshments, which consisted of cakes, dates, dried figs, and wines, and were handed around by the married ladies. About thirty minutes having been spent, in thus reviving the physical strength, the dance again commenced, and was continued, with great spirit and exertion, until a late hour of the night; when the weary, and drowsy guests retired; and there was an end to the biosterous fandango.

This was a collection of about the fairest samples, which the country could afford; and how far inferior were they, even to the unlearned and poorer classes, in our own country! Selfishness, it is true, is sure to make us have a good opinion of ourselves; and with ourselves, to make us appear favorable in comparison with others. A knowledge of this, should generally dictate to us, the propriety of not hazarding an expression, concerning our own goodness or greatness, in such a comparison: but there are instances, and this is one of them, in which there is no possibility of being mistaken. These very people, though they are not aware of it, in all their intercourse with foreigners, admit the inferiority of their judgment and knowledge, in every respect, except only in those things, which are immediately connected with their every day life. Why is there so great a difference? There must have been some great cause to have produced it: it is evident that such a difference did not exist, between the brave and enterprising, though infatuated Spaniards, who conquered Mexico; and our forefathers: even the people whom the Spaniards conquered, were far, very far superior to these. What great cause, we would enquire, has operated to sink them so far beneath their proud, daring, and high minded ancestors; and that too, while all the rest of the civilized world, has been moving forward with giant strides, up the great highway of human improvement? What could it have been, but "that accursed thirst for gold?"

But to plunge precipitately from one extreme to another, as has been usual with us, in the few preceding pages; to step, from the threshhold of the best specimen of society, which this degraded people possess, at once into the wilds of this wild country; we will enter again the Valley of the St. Wakine.

During our stay in the country, we went, in company with a friend, from Capt. Sutter's, to the South, in order to examine the St. Wakine; to see the wild horses, and to visit the Capital, Monte Rey. We proceeded down the Sacramento, passed around the head of the Bay, and came to the St. Wakine River, thirty miles above its mouth, on the third day. This part of the country is inhabited, by a very troublesome tribe of Indians, called the Horse Thieves, and contains no white settlement. The character of these Indians will readily be inferred from their name, which is most appropriate. They have long been hostile to the Spaniards, and a short time previous, had killed a white man ; and it was therefore necessary for us to be very cautious, while we were passing through their country. They have their Villages in the small valleys, and nooks, deep in the mountains ; where they keep their women and children, and to which they fly, as soon as they have committed any depredation. Among these fastnesses, they enjoy their booty in quiet : the Spaniards not daring to follow them among the mountains. They subsist, principally, upon horse-flesh ; some of which they procure from the wild bands, which cover the Valley of the St. Wakine, but principally, from the Spanish bands ; from which they frequently drive off hundreds, and sometimes thousands of horses. Many of these Horse Thieves have been educated in the Catholic Missions ; where they were comfortably fed and clothed, and promised homes, during their lives ; but when the Missions were broken up—by the avarice of the Spaniards ; these Indians fled to the mountains : from whence they have since continued to commit depredations, and destroy the lives and property, of their own enemies and destroyers.

Traveling up the St. Wakine, we frequently saw large herds of Elk and wild Horses. The Elk, which were often in herds of four or five hundred, were not very easily frightened, and seldom ran to a great distance ; but the Horses, which were still more numerous, and were scattered, in large bands, all along the river, after having satisfied themselves with approaching and examining us, would dash off across the valley, at full speed ; and, in their course whatever bands they came near, would join in the flight, until frequently, the plain would be covered, with thousands and thousands flying in a living flood towards the hills. Huge masses of dust hung upon their rear, and marked their track across the plain ; and even after they had passed entirely beyond the reach vision, we could still see the dust, which they were throwing in vast clouds into the air, moving over the highlands. These frightened bands were never out of sight ; so numerous are the wild horses on teh St. Wakine. Continuing up the river we came, on the second day, to a corál, which had been built some time previous, by our acquaintance, for the purpose of taking these wild horses. It was situated in a large slough of the river, at a part which was then dry, for several hundred yards; and was the principal crossing for the horses, from an island containing several thousand acres, which was formed by the slough. There were two large bands upon the island when we arrived, and we made an effort to drive them into the corál; but they took another crossing, and we did not succeed. Our friend pursued the first band that left the island, with the lassoo, endeavoring to take a fine mule, which he selected; but his horse being fatigued, he was not able to come up with it. When the second started, we put spur for the crossing which they were about to take, and arrived at the same time that the foremost horses of the band leaped down into the water. We endeavored to turn them, whooping and yelling most manfully, but those behind, urging those before, forced them forward, and they began to rush by. The pass was narrow, and the dust so obscured us, that they frequently ran near enough for us to strike them in the sides as they were passing; but we were at length compelled to retire, on account of the suffocating effect of the dust. Presently, again approaching, with whooping and yelling, we endeavored, the second time, to turn them; but they only gave way, and closed around us, and the dust again obliged us to retire: we finally succeeded in turning a few of the last, yet they were so determined to follow the others, that we only drove them a few hundred yards, towards the corál, before they plunged down a perpendicular bank, fifteen or twenty feet, into the slough, burying themselves completely under the water; aud gaining the opposite shore, followed the band. The Spaniards often take the wild horses in this manner, and frequently, by pursuing them, upon the open plain. When they have taken one, they confine it, with ropes, saddle it, put a halter on it, and having again loosened it, they mount, and ride it furiously, until it is completely exhausted. And they continue to do this, until the animal becomes tame, and tractable. These wild horses are of almost every color; some of them have a very fine appearance, but they are much smaller than well-bred horses; and their habits are, in some respects, entirely different from those of the domestic horses. From the corál, we proceeded across the country, to Monte Rey.

Arriving at Monte Rey, we found a gentleman and his family, who had left the States with us, and with whom, as we have before mentioned, we traveled, as far as Fort Hall. They left Fort Hall for California, under the pilotage of Captain Walker, about the same time that we left it, for the Falls of the Willammette. After traveling through the dreary country of which we have spoken, as far as the California Mountains, they followed that range South, several hundred miles, and entered the Valley of the St. Wakine, by Walker's Pass. The small supply of provisions; which, by very unpleasant means, they at length procured at Fort Hall, after continued and persevering effort; were exhausted, long before they could reach a place where they could be resupplied. A country so barren, as that through which they were compelled to travel, afforded, neither game, nor food of any kind, except that upon which the few miserable and beast like Indians, who inhabit that region, subsist—lizzards, crickets, ants, and the like—and which would, of course, be revolting to the palate of any other people, unless in the very extremity of starvation. They suffered extremely; and before they arrived at the Pass, they were driven to the necessity, of eating some of the mules and horses, which had served them so faithfully, and which were then poor, and worn out with fatigue, from long and laborious traveling, over a country so rough and barren. They left their wagons, and much of their baggage; and packing what they could, upon the remainder of their fatigued animals, they succeeded in gaining the Pass. When they came into the Valley of the St. Wakine, they fared more bountifully upon the wild horses, which they found in good condition, and in great abundance. They finally arrived, in the winter, at the settlements; and after suffering all hardships and privations, were prepared to relish, in no common degree, the abundance which they afforded.

We also, had an opportunity, during our stay in the country, of seeing most of those, with whom we parted at Fort Boisé, on Snake River. The gentleman in whose company we were at this time, was one of that party. They followed the route which they expected, at the time of our separation, to follow; experiencing, fortunately, not so much difficulty in finding it, as had been anticipated. Having left the head of the Malheur River, and traveled over a barren, sandy country, about two days, without water, they at length, after ascending a high mountain, came upon a lofty, but beautiful table land; rich, and wooded with pines, or varied by prairies, and coursed by many clear mountain streams. They discovered, what they supposed to be the head of the Willammette, and corrected an error, which had previously been entertained, concerning the source of the Sacramento. They had expected to endure suffering; and in this they were not mistaken.

Although they were fortunate, in finding their way through an unknown country, and still more so, in preserving their lives from its brutal and hostile inhabitants; yet the lateness of the season, together with their entire ignorance of a great portion of the pathless wilds, and precipitous mountains, over which they had to pass, subjected them to numerous, and serious hardships. At times, when they saw no way to move forward, an additional obstacle was opposed to their advancement, by heavy falls of snow; greatly increasing, and at the same time, concealing the dangers of their perilous way. Their provisions became exhausted. Some of their animals had been killed by the Indians, some dashed to pieces by falling from the rocks, and those that remained, poor from want of sufficient food, and worn down by the journey, were all upon which the little party had to depend for the support of life. After encountering delays, and suffering much from anxiety, fatigue, hunger, and cold, they at length succeeded in getting down into the Sacramento Valley. Thin and feeble themselves, they finally arrived, early in the winter, at Capt. Sutters; on foot, and leading their animals, which were no longer able to carry them. This was the point where they had designed, for a time, to terminate their travels; and here they found, that abundance, and repose, to which they had so long, and eagerly looked forward, and which their present condition so much required.

Almost all the suffering, which the emigrants to California experienced, was owing to the detention, which they were compelled to make along the road, for the purpose of supplying themselves with privisions. Had they been properly provided, before the commencement of the journey, and not depended at all on the game, they would have avoided it almost entirely. It is to be wondered at, that the person who assumed the leading of the party, and who was then making his second trip to California, had not learned, from his experience to give better counsel; but in respect to those who were unacquainted with the country, it is not in the least astonishing, that they should be mistaken, in making the necessary preparations, to travel comfortably, and securely, through a region so unlike every thing, to which they had ever been accustomed.

The Northern portion, of Western California, considered in comparison with the Mississippi Valley, like Oregon, contains a great deal less fertile land, in proportion to its extent. Much of this portion of California, which is far superior to any other, is taken up by mountains, or lands otherwise unfit for cultivation; whereas, in the Mississippi Valley, the whole might be brought into one vast, fruitful, and unbroken field. From this reason, the Mississippi Valley must always be the most productive, and wealthy country. But on account of the delightful mildness, and uniformity of the climate of California; it will forever be, the most healthy and happy country.

CHAPTER VI.

RETURN TO THE STATES.

JOURNEY FROM CAPTAIN SUTTER'S TO FORT HALL, WITH SOME OF ITS INCIDENTS.

Leave California for the United States—Difficulties in crossing Juba River—Extensive view from the summit of a mountain, with deep snow on one side, and naked earth and fine grass on the other—Burnt Mountains—Boiling Springs—Sink of Marie's River, and singular peculiarity of the stream—Encamp in the bend of the River, and have horses shot by the Indians—Travel over extensive wastes, and finally come to the Oregon Trail.

Having spent some months in exploring the country, and obtained a tolerably satisfactory knowledge, of the greater part of Northern or Upper California, either from personal observation, or by careful enquiries, from such persons as had made themselves acquainted with the various portions of the country, we determined on leaving for the United States. After much trouble and exertion in raising a small company of fifteen persons; on the 12th of May, 1845, we left Capt. Sutter's, on our homeward bound trip. We traveled up the Sacramento, on the East side, forty miles; and then traveled up Bear Creek—our course being about East. Crossing the east side of the Sacramento Valley, a distance of about twenty miles, we came to the spurs of the California Mountains. We continued to travel up through these hills, following the general course of the stream, until we came to its source; which is in a large marsh, greatly elevated above the Sacramento Valley. At this marsh we remained one day, in order to find a place where we could cross Juba River, which was a mile and a half distant, a stream of considerable size, very rapid, full of falls and canions, and was at this time quite high, from the melting of the snow on the mountains. It was only in a few places, where the hills were sufficiently gradual, to allow us to descend to the water; and these places were frequently between perpendicular falls, which were so near, and the velocity of the water so great, as to render the crossing very dangerous, if not absolutely impossible. This was the character of the first place where we struck the River, which was on the trail of a small emigrating company, that came into California, the previous summer. We had been told, by a gentleman whom we had met a few days before, returning from the mountains, where he had gone to get some wagons, and other property, which he had been compelled to leave, in the Fall, on account of the lateness of the season, and the fear of being blocked up by the coming snows, that it would be impossible for us to cross the stream, and that it would be best for us to return. We, however, discovered a place, where we ascended the mountain, immediately above us; and having, with much difficulty, on account of the steepness of the ascent, gained the summit; we followed the ridge—our progress being somewhat impeded by the snow—for about eight miles; and descended into a small bottom of the River. Traveling up the bottom about two miles, we came to a high, rocky spur, making into the water, around which we were at first unable to pass. But after searching and examing, for a long time, we at length found a place, where, by cutting away the brush for a considerable distance with our hatchets, and plunging through the mire and snow, we could pass around the spur. Having accomplished this, and traveled up the narrow bottom about two miles further, we again came to where the mountain neared the river. The bottom land was miry and covered with brush, and the snow was about four feet deep. Our loose animals, which were in front, were crowded into the stream by the pack animals, before we were aware of the situation. We succeeded, with difficulty, in stopping the animals which were packed with our provisions, &c., and stripping off our baggage and saddles, in the snow, we drove in the rest of our animals. They all succeeded in gaining a small island, near the opposite shore, just large enough to contain them; where they stayed the whole night in the snow, without anything to eat. Having kindled a large fire, and arranged our camp, our next object was, to make a way, by which we could cross ourselves and baggage. For this purpose, we felled a tree, which not being long enough to reach, was carried down the stream: we then selected a large tall Fir, which we cut about half off, and left it until the next morning, when we finished cutting it down. In falling, it broke in two, about fifteen feet from the opposite shore, and the top was carried away; the main trunk, however, lodged against the upper part of a large rock, and the force of the current supported it above. From the broken end of this tree, we were able to throw poles across to the opposite shore, and in this manner we constructed a way, upon which we carried across our baggage.

Having repacked our horses, we continued up Juba River, traveling about an East course; sometimes in the narrow bottom of the stream, and sometimes upon the sides and summits of the ridges. The snow still continued deep, and covered both the bottoms and the mountains, in all parts, around us; but it was very compact, and in the morning would generally bear our animals. We traveled up the North side about eleven miles, and came to the forks of the stream; the North branch of which we crossed with difficulty, the current being very strong, and the channel full of large rocks, upon which some of our pack animals fell; and were carried down the stream: and we were compelled, to leap into the water, just melted from the snow, and assist them to the shore. Having crossed, we came into a prairie, about one mile in width, and three or four in length, extending to the base of the main ridge of the mountain; which now lay immediately before us. We ascended this ridge without much labor, although it was composed entirely of granite, which lay in large detached fragments, over the whole surface: and gained the summit. This, on either side of the narrow gap through which we passed, was very sharp, and perfectly bald and barren. Immediately upon reaching the summit, the whole Eastern side of the mountain burst upon the view; and a sudden thrill of joy, awakened in every bosom, and flashed in every eye: for the snow which had so much impeded, and made so disagreeable and dangerous, the ascent on the West, had melted almost entirely away, on the East. Down the mountain we could see a green spot, at the further end of a beautiful lake, which spread out in a broad crystal sheet below us. But although this was so pleasing to us, as it was now the third day since our animals had had any nourishment, we could not but remain, for a moment, to admire and enjoy the vastness of the prospect around us. On either side, there was no limit to the vision, save the thickning air of the distant horizon, which bent down, and rested upon the far off hills, like the bending sky, upon the bosom of the great deep. Within this wide range, was a succession of mountain after mountain, increasing in height, as they approached the summit, upon which we stood. To the West, from whence we came, wherever we could see through the tall forests, all was wrapped in one unbroken sheet of snow; to the East, whither we were going, we looked down, down, until the eye was lost among the dimly descried, crowded, and confused objects in the distance.

Descending the Eastern declivity, we came to the lake, and passed around on the Northern side, to the further extremity, where we found the grass, which we had seen from the summit of the mountain, in abundance, and of a very good quality. We remained at this place the rest of the day, in order to refresh our animals, which were by this time much exhausted, and fatigued, from hunger, and plunging through the snow. The distance from the forks of Juba River to the lake, is about ten miles; and in this lake the South branch of Truckies River has its source. This stream was called, by the emigrating party that went into California, in the Fall of 1844, after the name of an Indian, who piloted them across the mountains.

Leaving the lake, and the river which flows from it, to the right, we bore off to the North East, for a wide, deep gap, through which we supposed that we could both pass, and leave the mountains. At ten miles, we crossed the North branch of Truckies River, a stream of considerable size. We traveled eight miles further, to the head of a stream, running to the North West, which we called Snow River; as a heavy fall of snow, here obscuring our course, compelled us to halt. Snow continued to fall during this, and the succeeding day; and we remained in camp. When it ceased, we again proceeded on our journey, leaving the gap for which we had been steering, and bearing to the East, through a break in the mountain which follows the course of Truckies River, and which is a spur of the main California chain. Having crossed this mountain, we again came, at five miles, to Truckies River, which we crossed and traveled down on the South side—passed across a barren plain, ten miles in width, and at fifteen miles, came to the Burnt Mountains. These are a succession of several high, perfectly barren, and very rocky ridges. The distance across, is about thirty-five miles, and the way was very tedious and toilsome.

We found the Indians on Truckies River, generally, very wild, entirely naked, and miserably poor. They live in floating houses, constructed of long, coarse grass, on rafts of dry willow brush. They are armed with bows and arrows, and subsist, almost entirely, on lizzards, crickets, and muscles.

Having crossed the Burnt Mountains, we found that it would be necessary for us to leave Truckies River, as it now bore too much to the North: and accordingly, we remained one day encamped, in order to rest our animals, for a hard travel, across a sandy, unproductive plain, thirty-five miles, to the sink of Marie's River;

which distance was without drinkable water. We passed three springs in the plain, but the first was salt. and the other two, which were close together, were both hot; the largest one, which was ten feet in diameter, was boiling furiously; and we could see the steam arising from it, several miles. These springs rise through volcanic rock; and large fragments of the same are scattered over the ground, around them.

At the sink of Marie's River, the stream is lost in the sand. This sink is a large sandy marsh, about three miles wide, and ten miles long, full of bull-rushes, and very miry; the water which it contains, is also warm, and has a very disagreeable taste. From this point, we traveled up Marie's River, which flows from North East to the South West, through a sandy plain, almost entirely destitute of vegetation. This plain is about twenty miles wide, and is bordered on each side, by high, rugged, and perfectly barren mountains. On the lower part of the River, we could find but little grass for our animals, and we had traveled two hundred miles up it, before we found water, coming in on either side. Unlike any other stream, perhaps, it is larger in the middle than any where else; it continued to increase in size as we proceeded up, until we came to where it receives its last tributary. Here we encamped, one night, in the bend of the river, which we used as a corál, the guard standing at the entrance. During the night, the animals made several attempts to rush by the guard; and it was with the greatest difficulty, that they were able to keep them. In the morning, we were astonished to find four of them fatally wounded; they had been shot by the Indians, who had swam across in the night; we also found several arrows in the encampment, some of which had evidently been shot at the men. We left one of the animals dead, in camp, and another was able to go only a half a mile. The Indians had killed them to eat, and we were determined to disappoint them as much as possible, by driving those that were able to travel, away. After we had packed up, two of us remained behind; and the rest of the company proceeded, taking all the animals. We then concealed ourselves in the brush, intending to kill, if we could, whoever came to the dead beast. The company had been gone about two hours, when we saw an Indian coming towards us. He came within about two hundred and fifty yards of the point of brush, in which we were concealed; but think-thinking this rather a long shot, we let him pass, supposing that he would return to the horse, after having examined the company's trail, which he seemed to be doing; he was, however, in all probability, suspicious, and went away, and we saw nothing more of him, or any other Indians. Having waited half an hour longer, and finding that he did not return, we left our place of concealment, and followed the company, three of whom we met, after having gone about five miles, returning with our horses, to meet us.

Overtaking our companions, we continued to travel up the river, finding now an abundance of grass in its bottoms and on its tributaries; which were still very rare. Fifty miles above our unfortunate encampment, we left the river, and the last of our wounded animals. About the head of Marie's River, there is a large extent of country covered with a superior quality of grass; the stalks, branching out into numerous heads, are loaded with seeds, which are highly nutritious.

Leaving the valley, we crossed the spur of a mountain, which was also covered with grass, and came to waters running North, towards Snake River; and for fifty miles, the country over which we traveled, afforded excellent grazing. At the termination of this distance, we came to a spot, containing several acres, full of small pools of hot water. From these hot pools, we traveled over a mountainous country, leaving the main range, which was broken in several places, by deep gaps, several miles to the left, and between us and the Valley of Snake River. The grass became less abundant, and as we advanced, a great portion of the country became quite barren.

At one hundred miles from the Hot Pools, we came to and crossed the Raft River, which empties into Snake River, twenty three miles below the American Falls. Thence we crossed the main range of mountains, South of the Valley of Snake River, through a large, deep gap, and at thirty miles came to the river, five miles below the junction of the Portneiff; thence we proceeded to Fort Hall, a distance of twenty three miles, where we arrived on the 20th day of June, forty days having elapsed since we left Capt. Sutter's, in California.

In the whole country between the Eastern base of the California Mountains, and Fort Hall, we saw no game, of any description, excepting a few Antelopes, on the head of Marie's River. The greater portion of the country, after leaving the head waters of the Sacramento, is either broken by mountains, or covered with extensive wastes of sand and volcanic desolation; and can never be inhabited, by a people much superior to the insect and reptile eating savages, found at the present time upon some of its streams.

Here we will leave, for a time, the Company from California; return to the Falls of the Willammette; and follow, from that place, the Oregon Company, until the time when the two, having accidentally met in the mountains, united.*

*For the sake of uniformity of expression, "we" has been used throughout the previous pages, although it will be perceived by a reference to the introduction, that only Mr. WINTER was in California.

CHAPTER VI.

RETURN TO THE STATES.

JOURNEY FROM OREGON CITY TO THE WESTERN PART OF THE STATE OF MISSOURI, WITH SOME OF ITS INCIDENTS.

Return from Oregon City to the United States—Difficulty with the Walawala Indians, and timely intervention of Capt. Grant—Meet with Wm. H. Winter, on his return from California, near Fort Hall—Difficulty with the Pawnees—Came to the Western settlements of the United States.

On the 19th day of April, 1845, we left Oregon City, for the United States. Our company, consisting of twelve persons, proceeded, a part by land, with the animals, and a part by water, with the baggage and provisions. And as the Cascade Mountains were yet impassable, on account of the snow, it was necessary for those who went by land, to follow the Columbia River: to do this, they were compelled to cross over to the North side at Vancouver, and a part of them re-crossed above the Falls of the Columbia. They had only a dim Indian trail to follow, which frequently wound along between rocky precipices and the river; it was sometimes covered with water, and a great portion of it was over loose fragments of rock, and along the sides of very steep hills and mountains. The streams which empty into the Columbia, were full, and all conspired to make the way through the Cascade Mountains, by land, very difficult. The passage by water was, likewise, somewhat impeded by high winds, strong currents, and the portage around the Falls. We arrived at the Wascopin Mission on the 1st of May, where we left our canoes, and packed the baggage upon our horses. We remained here one day, during which time Mr. Brewer and his lady, who are connected with the Mission, did every thing in their power to assist us, and make our stay agreeable. From the Mission, we followed the South bank of the Columbia to Fort Walawala.

We found the De Chutes and John Day's Rivers too deep to ford, and were compelled to employ the Indians to take us across them, in their canoes. When we came to John Day's River, it was late, and we encamped. We had been previously informed by the Indians, in case we should find no person here, that if we would go down to the bank of the Columbia and fire a gun, those who were on the opposite side, would come over and assist us. Finding no one where the the trail crossed the river, in the morning, one of our party mounted his horse, and rode down to the Columbia; intending, if he found no one there, to make the signal which we had been instructed to give. But finding Indians on the same side we were on, he attempted to make a bargain with them. They pretended at first, not to understand the language which he spoke, (Chenook,) but gave him to understand that they had no canoes. After spending some minutes, endeavoring to pursuade them to do something for us, an old man walked up to him, grasped his horse firmly by the bridle, and made signs to him to dismount; at the same time, a squaw came out of the lodge with a large knife, and stood before him. He kicked at the Indian, and tried to rein his horse away, but was unable to release himself. He then drew a pistol from his belt, cocked it, and threw the muzzle against the Indians breast; at which, letting go his hold on the horse, and extending his arms, he sprang back, with an exclamation of terror, to the door of the hut, and protested that he meant no harm and was only sporting. He saw no arms, and intended first to rob the man of his horse; and having succeeded in that, to strip him, probably, of every thing he had. He did not know that the buckskin coat concealed a pistol, or that there were friends at hand. In a short time, the rest of us having packed up, followed down to where the Indians were; they soon found their canoes, set us over the stream on our own terms, and became exceedingly friendly and accommodating.

They are always very pleasant and harmless in the presence of a superior force, with this unvarying exception; they will always steal any thing and every thing they can lay their hands on, when they think there is a possibility of concealing, or carrying it away, without being detected. But where they have the power, their disposition immediately changes; they are then frowning and insolent; and not satisfied with pilfering, they frequently commit open robberies. Many instances of this have occurred with small companies of emigrants, on their way down the Columbia; who, having imprudently separated themselves from the larger companies, and probably parted with their arms, have, some of them, been plundered; some of them stripped of a good part of their clothing, some have been whipped, and others, have been otherwise insulted, and abused. We heard of an instance, where two men, who were descending the Columbia River in a canoe, landed, for some purpose, at an Indian village; and while on shore, an Indian came up to one of the men, with a dead snake in his hands, which he was pleased to draw several times across the white man's face. There are those who would not have borne such an insult tamely. but it would have been dangerous to have resented. They have frequently amused themselves, by brandishing their arms in people's faces, or presenting them with their drawn bows. They have never yet taken the life of an emigrant; but, unless they are soon checked, their insolence will grow to something of a more serious nature.

Having arrived at Fort Walawala, we learned that an Italian priest, Father Soderena, then at the Calespel Mission, was exceedingly anxious to return to the United States; and as we were weak, and glad to receive any addition to our numbers, we consented to wait until a messenger, who was instantly dispatched from the Fort, could inform him of our presence, and that we were on our return to the United States. There being but little grass near the Fort, and several of the party wishing to trade horses with the Indians, we moved a few miles beyond Dr. Whitman's Mission, (twenty-five miles from the Fort,) and encamped. Intending to turn our stay to the best advantage, by resting and recruiting our animals, we were careful to select an encampment, where there was excellent pasturage, and good water, in immediate connection.

While we were encamped in the neighborhood of the Mission, a party of twenty or thirty Chiefs and braves, a deputation from the Walawala, Nez Pierce, and Kious Indians, came, and met in council with Dr. Whitman, Mr. Spaulding, and other gentlemen connected with the Mission. They told the Missionaries that the hearts of some of their people were bad; and the object of the council proved to be a trial, to ascertain whether Dr. Whitman was not worthy of death. The charges brought against the Doctor were these: Yellow Serpent, a Chief of the Walawalas, together with his son, and a number of his people, went into California in the Autumn previous, to the time of this council, taking with them a band of horses, which they intended to trade for cattle during the Winter, and return in the Spring. While they were in California, a difficulty arose between Elijah—which was the name of the Yellow

Serpent's son—and an American, concerning a mule which Elijah said he had caught among the wild horses. The American claimed the mule, and a quarrel ensued. Afterwards, while they were disputing about the matter, Elijah went away, and got his gun, for the purpose, as his people said, of shooting a hawk. The American supposed, or at least he said that he was sure the gun was intended for him; and taking the hint, withdrew immediately. This happened in the camp of the Walawalas.

On the following day, Elijah came to Captain Sutter's Fort, where the American was; who, as soon as he saw the Indian enter, determined upon an immediate and more than savage revenge. Taking his gun, he entered the room where the Indian was sitting, presented the muzzle to his breast, and told him to prepare to die. No explanation or defence was permitted. It was said, that the Indian, who professed Christianity, kneeled to pray; and that, while engaged in that act of final preparation for another world, he was shot dead by the American. He was killed in the presence of his father, who, flying from the Fort, collected his people instantly, and hastened out of the country. They left a great portion of their property, which they feared to take time to collect; and although it was in the Winter, they rushed on, over mountains and snows, and through the files and ambuscades of other hostile tribes, and came, after suffering great loss of property, into their own country. This affair was frowned upon by almost the whole white population of Oregon. There were few persons in the country, unfriendly to the Indian who had been killed. And a letter was dispatched by the authorities, to the friends of the deceased, and Chiefs of his tribe, offering their services, whenever a favorable opportunity would present, to regain the property, and bring the offender to justice. The son of the Yellow Serpent, had been taught at the Mission, by Dr. Whitman, and had always been on terms of most intimate friendship with him. But because his son had been killed by an American in California, the Walawala Chief demanded the life of Dr. Whitman. He argued that it would be no more than just and equal, since his son was a preacher, to take the life of a preacher for satisfaction. This equivalent they all considered, must be given, in order to make the hearts of their people good.

In addition to this, they accused him of another crime; which was, that two Snake Diggers—Indians, living on the lower part of

Snake River, East of the Blue Mountains—had lately been killed by Americans. This was made an important item in the charge, although they were not on very friendly terms with the Snake Indians. The circumstances of this affair, were thus: Two Americans, who had remained at one of the trading posts, in the mountains, through the Winter, were coming down to the settlements on Willammette. While traveling up the Brulé River, their horses were taken, in the night, from their encampment; and in the morning, they found themselves on foot, far from any Fort, Mission, or settlement; surrounded by mountains, in the midst of an unfeeling people, and without the means of carrying their baggage and provisions. In this situation, they determined to follow the Indians, and regain, if possible, the horses that had been stolen. Arming themselves with all the weapons they had; they proceeded on the track of the horses. They passed by, where one had been killed, and after several hours of rapid pursuit, came up with the thieves. They found them, with the flesh of the horse they had killed, packed upon the other. They attempted flight, but the horse was so loaded that it could not run; and rather than surrender their stolen property, they presented their guns, and offered battle. Sadly to their discomfiture, their fusees refused to be discharged; but the rifles of the Americans, were sure and deadly: both of the Indians remaining with the horse, fell when they reported, yelled, and died. The Americans returned to their encampment, with the horse, placed upon him their baggage and provisions, and proceeded for Dr. Whitman's, where they at length arrived in safety.

They were allowed to lodge in one of the Mission houses, and to eat at the Doctor's table. This the council also regarded as a crime. But their object, however, was not to punish; it was rather to have an equivalent. They only wished that the Americans should suffer a loss, as great as their own. Dr. Whitman reasoned with them, and appealed to them, by every means, which he thought would tend, in the least, to affect them in his favor; and so did all the others; but it was in vain. After a long consultation, by which they appeared to be not the least shaken in their opinions, they went away, saying that they themselves, would not disturb the Missionaries; but, that they could not help, what their young men might do. After the council was ended, several of our party, who were present, expressed their opinions to the the gentlemen of the Mission; saying, that they considered it, both imprudent, and wrong in them, to hazard their own lives, and the lives of their families, by remaining longer among these people. Dr. Whitman, who is naturally a man of excellent judgment, and especially so with regard to mattters relating to the Indians, and who is, moreover, not to be frightened where there is no cause to fear, replied, that he also believed, that prudence, and their safety, required that they should abandon the Mission, for a time, at least. The same opinion was expressed, by all the other gentlemen.

Whether there were other causes to excite the Indians to this step, besides those which they made known, is uncertain. We would hope, that men professing to love good feeling and good actions; claiming to be engaged in the same great cause of Christianizing, and civilizing an ignorant, and barbarous people, would not, merely because they belonged to different sects, or denominations, aim at each other's success, by such vile, uncharitable means. This, and the Catholic Mission on the upper Columbia, are on very unfriendly terms. We would not give it as our opinion, that these unfriendly feelings have been carried to such an extreme; but, there are thousands of instances, in which those professing to be Christians, have acted towards each other, even as unchristianly.

A good body of soldiers, garisoned in the Walawala Valley, would not only be of great benefit in protecting the emigrants, and whoever else might wish to pass through that country, but also to the Indians themselves. For such a garison would keep them in awe, and thereby prevent them from committing depredations, for which they would afterwards have to be punished. They would, at the same time, protect the rights of the Indians, prevent feuds from arising between them and the white people, and establish a peace, and friendship, which would likely be lasting, and beneficial to both; favorable to the civilization of the Indians, and to the promulgation, and extension of Christain principles, among them.

Shortly after this occurred, we removed to a small farm, belonging to Mr. McKenley, the Principal at Fort Walawala; situated on the Hudson's Bay Company's trail to Fort Hall. While we awaited here, the arrival of the Priest, who would come in company with Capt. Grant, (then going up to Fort Hall, with a party, and a large supply of goods and flour,) the Chief of the Walawalas, one evening, came to our camp, with about a dozen men. Without saying a word, or noticing us when we spoke to him, he rode between our fires, where we were cooking, and our baggage; which were only a few feet apart. We told him to go away; that he was throwing the dust in our victuals; but he seemed not to hear. He then reined his horse short around one of the fires, and came near riding over the vessels in which one of the men was preparing supper. He was told repeatedly to go away, but was still silent, and heedless. The person who was cooking at the fire, then took hold of the horse, and endeavored to lead it away; but the Indian pulled against him, and would not allow the horse to move. He at last took up a stick, struck the horse, and drove it out. At this, the Chief became greatly enraged; talked loudly, and threateningly: he would hear nothing; and at length went away in the same mood. Some of the party were a little uneasy; but the night passed, and we thought but little more of it.

We learned that Capt. Grant was near, and sent a messenger, to tell the Priest, that we would move the next day, and to request him to join us as soon as possible. The messenger returned, and informed us, that he had agreed that we should encamp the next night, at a certain place, with Capt. Grant; where the Priest would complete his arrangements, and be ready to proceed with us. We accordingly packed up and started, with the intention of going to the place agreed on. We, however, missed our road, and after having gone eight or ten miles, halted to take dinner.

We had just arranged our baggage, &c., and had our animals grazing near, when we noticed a cloud of dust, away in the direction from which we came. In a few minutes we perceived that it was approaching us; and in a very short time more, we saw that it was nearing us very rapidly: and then heard shouting. We were convinced that it was the Yellow Serpent, coming to revenge the insult, which he had forced from us; and no doubt, for the purpose of having an excuse, for making this attack. We hastened to construct a frail breastwork of our packs; the only materials we had, out of which we could form something to shield us from the balls and arrows of the rapidly approaching foe. But we had not finished our work, before Capt. Grant, who had seen the Indians coming, and guessed their object, in company with the Priest, and Mr. Ramo, a Frenchman, and overseer of the camp, came up to us at full speed, from nearly the same direction, and a few hundred yards ahead of the Indians. Mr. Grant, we knew, had spent a great portion of his life among these people, had a powerful influence over them, and was perfectly acquainted with their character and manners. He advised us to lay aside our arms, assume a careless demeanor, and trust the event to him; assuring us, at the same time, that he was confident he could make peace, without any loss of life or property; both of which were of nearly equal importance to us, in the situation we then were. There was no time for words, and we yielded to his judgment, superior in such affairs to ours, and followed his advice. The Indians, about sixty in number, came yelling, and beating loudly on a kind of a drum. When within three hundred yards, they separated; the Chief, with one part, charged up, on the same side of the little stream on which we were encamped, yelling and flourishing their arms, and firing in the air; while the others, on the opposite side, with the same kind of music, swept away our animals. The Chief, with his party, reined up against our packs, and formed in a circle around us; except a few, who continued to fly back and foward, within eight or ten yards of us, yelling, firing and flourishing their arms. At this instant a hot headed Southerner, seizing his gun, and crying out that we were betrayed and should sell our lives as dearly as possible, was just in the act of firing on one of these yelling theives, but was prevented, by the intervention of some of our party, and the remonstrance of Capt. Grant. Thus they stood around us, half naked, painted in the most hidious manner, and with their arms ready in their hands. The other Indians, having driven our horses beyond the hills, and performed a war dance, on one of the neighboring summits, at a signal given by those in our camp, came charging down with whoop and yell, and thickened the ranks around us. Our situation was uncertain; the Chief and Capt. Grant, with the Frenchman, were engaged in an excited parley, the event of which, we did not know. From the great disparity in numbers, we were perfectly in the power of our foes, who could have crushed us in an instant, with a single blow; which any act or expression of rashness, or want of boldness, would probably have brought about.

But the most affecting scene which our confused camp presented, was that of two little girls, who, trembling with fear, and in tears, crouched at their father's feet, seemed to implore that protection from a parent which he could not give. To feel one's self in the power of a mean and miserable foe, whom he despises, is maddening; and when so surrounded, powerless, and submissive, we could not but dream of vengeance, as we looked about us, and hope to crush, at some sweet future period, those grim frowning wretches. After a long consultation, in which the Serpent refered to the death of his son, and to the two Shoshonees. (Snakes.) that had been killed, forgetting the many injuries, robberies, and insults, which emigrants from the United States had suffered from his people; he agreed to consider the insult canceled, to return our horses, and withdraw peaceably, without interrupting us or our property, upon Capt. Grant promising to give him a green blanket, and some tobacco. They kept their faith towards us, but not towards our property; taking advantage of their proximity, and the disorder, to pilfer whatever they could lay their hands on. Having regained our animals, and packed up, we followed Capt. Grant, and joined his camp in the evening. This circumstance happened on the 20th of May. Having joined with Capt. Grant, we continued to travel with him, until we reached his Fort.

At our second encampment on the Brulé River, a Frenchman and his Indian wife came to us, from Fort Boisé. They came expressly to meet Capt. Grant, having, probably, some message. The Frenchman told us, that the village near the mouth of the river, exasperated against the white people, on account of the death of their friends, would hardly allow him to pass. They debated among themselves whether they should not kill him; but by the intervention of his wife, who was of their tribe, and related to some of the Indians of the village, and as he was not an American, they concluded to spare him. We were aware, that if we met any of these Indians, they would not be well disposed towards us; but this timely information put us more on our guard.

On the 30th of May, we crossed the Brulé River, at the village of the unfriendly Indians. The women and children had fled from their huts, as soon as they became apprised of our approach; and here and there on the hills around, we could see them couched among the sage. They knew that we were Americans, and the men, standing around in groups, regarded us with angry, and sullen countenances. But under the circumstances, they were more in fear than we were, and appeared without their arms. As we passed, the relations of the two that had been killed, set up a howl of lamentation, which they continued as far as we could hear.

That evening, we pitched our camps on the bank of Snake River, three miles distant from the village. Many of the Diggers came into our encampment, and appeared to be anxious to obtain some opportunity of revenge. Some of them were carrying their arms, and some had their faces striped, and spotted, with black and white, the colors of war. Some of them were also harranging loudly about their misfortune, and telling how bad the Americans were, and how very bad were their own hearts. In the evening, Capt. Grant said to them, through his interpreter, that, as his countrymen and our's were friendly, and as we had been traveling together, we were then, all like one people, and that whatever act they committed against one, would be felt equally by the other, and treated accordingly. At dusk, we brought our animals close, and tied them up, between the line of our camps and the River. During the night, we kept up a vigilent guard, and fortunately were not disturbed.

On the 1st of June, we arrived opposite Fort Boisé, where we remained four days, while Capt. Grant was re-arranging, and disposing of some of his packs. The Diggers followed us here from their village on the Brulé. By this time, it was generally known by the Indians in the neighborhood, that there was a small party of Americans in their country; and their numbers increasing, about our camp, gave us reason to suppose, that they still cherished some hostile intention. We had little fear for our personal safety, but were somewhat uneasy on account of our animals. We were confident, that if they undertook to take them in the night, we must loose part, at least.

In the evening, Capt. Grant again addressed them, through his interpreter. In summing up their grievances, they accused one of the last Emigration, who had his horses stolen, of taking others in their stead, from an innocent Indian; and complained, that is was very bad, in that American, to make one man suffer for what another had done. "Very true," replied the Captain; "I am glad to "find you agreeing with me. That was a bad man, and you "would be equally so, were you to make these men, who have never "injured you, suffer, in any way, for the wrongs and losses you have "received from others." To this they would not reply, and he continued: "He who took your horses, I say, was a bad man, but "the men who killed your people did well. Those who were killed "were thieves, and they deserved to die. Do you act as they act- "ed, and you shall be treated in the same manner. If you wish to "steal any of these horses, it is good. Come this very night. "You will find many of them loose on the prairie, far from our "camps. Those only that are swift and strong, we will keep here. "You need not come for them; we never sleep. But remember

"this: if you come, wherever you go, we will follow you. If, in
"the morning, one of our horses is missing, we will follow you.
"We will not only retake our own, but will drive away your's also.
"We will not be content with destroying your villages; but, in
"order to rid ourselves, and every one else, of such thieves and
"pests, we will wipe you from the face of the earth. Go away
"now, and come to-night if you wish. But remember; I have but
"one tongue. I talk straight."

The Indians took him at his word. Our horses, excepting a few, were allowed to wander, unguarded, over the prairie, but none of them were disturbed. These people afterwards brought us fish, and whatever else they had to sell, and we traded with them. They appeared to have abandoned all idea of disturbing us, and we had no more difficulty with them.

On the 6th of June, we left Fort Boisé, and traveled up Snake River, on the South side.

On the 8th, we noticed a Comet in the North West. We observed it with a common spy glass, and it was so distinct, that we could not be mistaken. It continued to appear, in the same quarter, for many days.

On the 10th, at the middle of the day, we came to the place, where emigrants generally cross over to the North side of the river. There was some demand in our camp for horse-shoes and horse-shoe nails, and one of the party, who reported himself to be an excellent swimmer, and at the same time, something of a brave, had been saying for several days previous, that he knew where a large lot of such articles had been buried on an island, at this crossing, and promised, besides, when we came to the place, to swim over and get them. We now reminded him of his promise. He hesitated a little, but finally consented, by another person agreeing to accompany him. It was but a short swim to the island, and the person who went with him made it easily; but he, when he had got about two thirds of the way over, became frightened, strangled, and called for help. His companion in the enterprise, assisted him to the shore, and he began to search for the hidden treasures: but time had obliterated the marks, either from the place, or from his memory; and the search was in vain. His companion became satisfied, in a few minutes, and returned; but he who was the leader in the enterprise, and was such an excellent swimmer, and above all, who was so brave, shrank from the dangers of another voyage. He had now, neither confidence in his craft, nor crew. He was lame in his arm, subject to the cramp, short winded, and withal, a little afraid. He was in a sad condition, perfectly naked, while the rays of a mid-day sun, were pouring down with a withering intensity. In the shade, he was literally covered with hungry musquetoes; and out of it, he was blistered by the excessive heat of the sun. It was an hour, before an Indian could get horses to bring him off; and during this time, he enjoyed all the luxuries, and comforts, of his solitary situation, uninterrupted, undivided, and unenvied. When he returned, we received him as the Robinson Crusoe of the camp; and the Island, in commemoration of the event, was afterwards the Juan Fernandez of the Desert.

We continued on our way, without interruption, or occurrence worthy of notice; traveling about twenty miles each day; and on the 17th, arrived at Fort Hall. Here, and in the camp of Capt. Grant, we received every assistance, attention, and respect, which it was in his power to give, or we could desire; contrary to the treatment we formerly received from him, while on our way to Oregon. For this kindness and attention, under such circumstances as those in which we were often placed, we will ever feel the deepest sense of gratitude, and consider ourselves, under obligations of no common kind. In this, we are confident, that we express the sentiments, not only of ourselves, but of every individual in the company. Yet, while we remember these kindnesses, with the warmest feelings, justice forbids that we should forget entirely that other treatment, so contrary.

We remained at Fort Hall one day, in order to rest our animals, and have the company of a Mexican, who would conduct us by the shortest route, to the camp of Messrs. Vasques and Smith, (Peg Leg,) where we hoped to have some addition to our company. We received a letter at the Fort, written from their camp, and addressed to any Company, returning from Oregon to the United States; stating that there were several persons there, who wished to go down by the first opportunity, and requesting us to come that way. We were informed that they had probably gone, but our anxiety to receive any addition to our numbers, urged us to leave nothing doubtful.

Our company, excepting two, left Fort Hall on the 19th, for the Soda Springs. We delayed nearly one day, on the way, waiting for the two men who were behind; but becoming impatient, we determined to proceed to that point, by which, we knew they would have to pass. When we came to the Springs, we found that they had arrived already, and were waiting for us. We had prepared ourselves to talk hard to them, for causing us delay, but the information which they brought, was ample to shield them from our displeasure. There was a company behind, from California.

They were near, and we, of course, halted until they came up. We were soon to enter a country, inhabited by a powerful, warlike, and hostile tribe of Indians, the Sioux; and it was with no small degree of mutual pleasure to us, that a kind Providence, guiding and guarding, was pleased to unite our small and inefficient forces; which, when thus united, amounted to only twenty-six persons. Under such circumstances, especially, as it brought together friends and acquaintances who had passed life's earliest and most cherished scenes together, and who, before, had long been ignorant even of the existence of each other. And the event was more thrilling and impressive, as it occurred in such a wild, gloomy, barren, and savage country, far away from home and friends, where the human kind was seldom seen, and when they were, most generally avoided. We will not describe the scene, but leave it to the imagination of those who are not destitute of sensibility, and who cannot but appreciate, in some degree, the feelings which were awakened, by such an occasion.

On the 22d of June, the two companies united, and proceeded, by moderate traveling, to the camp of Vasques and Peg Leg; the former of whom, had left his trading house, for fear of the Sioux and Shians. We found them several miles from the emigrant's trail, on one of the branches of Green River; and, as many of our animals were much fatigued and reduced, we determined to remain several days.

We found, upon arriving at this place, that those persons who wrote the letter, which we received at Fort Hall, had met with a company of traders, and had been gone about twenty days. While remaining here, we were entertained by accounts of all the parties that ever had been cut to pieces by the Sioux, all the difficulties and dangers which the white men, living in the mountains, had ever encountered by them, and probably a great many more. We passed, here, the 4th of July, and on the 5th, again proceeded.

Having crossed Green River, by rafting and swimming, on the 7th of July; in the morning, of the succeeding day, we met the van of a large Emigration, from whom we learned some of the principal events, which had occurred in the States, during the past year; among which, was the election of Mr. Polk to the Presidency.

In a few days after we had met the Emigration, several of our party, anxious to travel faster than was deemed prudent by the majority, and unwilling to yield their own opinions, separating from the company, proceeded ahead. It is strange, that men so surrounded, on every hand, with danger, and at the same time perfectly conscious of their situation, should allow little trivial differences of opinion, to separate them; exposing their lives on account of a mere whim, which, at most, does not profess any benefit, worthy of consideration. But it is so here. If a company is strong and united, there is no security that it will long continue so; if it is weak to-day, it is no reason that it will not be weaker to-morrow.

We found the Emigration scattered near five hundred miles, and the number of persons composing it, were about three thousand. They were in fine spirits, and high hopes, and far ahead of either of the Emigrations who had gone previously. We found Buffalo on Sweet Water, where we were able, by halting a few days, to recruit our stock of provisions.

On the 21st, we met a Mr. Sublet, brother to the celebrated mountaineer, William Sublet, who informed us, that there was a large party of Sioux, somewhere below, in the vicinity of the North Fork, and near the trail; and that eight of them, a few days before had pursued one of their hunters, within a short distance of their camp. He gave, as his opinion, that it would be impossible for us to pass them without their seeing us, and that if they saw us, they would take our horses, and perhaps our hair, unless we could beat them in a fight. We were only seventeen men, and to complete the consolation, there were, probably, about eighty lodges of Sioux; with which there would be about seven hundred warriors. We had no alternative, but to proceed with caution. We sometimes traveled in the night, and always smothered our camp fires before it grew dark; prevented all unnecessary firing of guns, made our encampments as secluded as possible, and kept the strictest watch, both day and night. Under such circumstances, it was easy to make an Indian spy out of a rock, or a charging war party out of a whirlwind. We saw their trail, but Providence, our caution, or their absence, prevented us from seeing them, and them from seeing us.

We arrived at Fort Lauramie, without molestation or difficulty, on the 27th of July. Here we were doomed to suffer another very great diminution in our numbers. The majority of our little company, having become tired of long traveling, determined to dispose of their animals, and enjoy a few days of repose, in a place where they would be confident of security, and free from the toil and anxiety attendant upon our perilous way. Their intention was to go across to Fort St. Peters, on the Missouri River, in connection with the American Fur Company's wagons which were to start in a short time, with Buffalo robes, for that place. The Trading Companies here, had undertaken to send their robes down the Platte River in boats, but the River falling, left the broad channel almost without water, and their scows dry upon the sand. They were therefore compelled to persue some other course. The American Fur Company were hauling back the loading of their boats to Fort Laurimie, whence they would take it, in some manner, across the country to Fort St. Peters, and thence, in batteaux, down the Missouri River to St. Louis. The other Company would take their's by land, directly to Independence. From Fort St. Peters, our companions were promised a passage on board the Fur Company's boats, to whatever point on the Missouri they wished. They arrived in the States, as we afterwards learned, in safety, but later, by about a month, than we who came directly by land.

Our little company, now dwindled down to seven persons, had yet to travel between seven and eight hundred miles, according to our estimate of the distance, through an Indian country: yet the reflection that we had passed over the most dangerous part of our way unharmed, gave us confidence to believe that the same protecting Providence would guide us on and guard us as before.

The Sioux and Shians, who, next to the Black Feet, are the terror of the mountains, and the tribes which had been the cause of our greatest dread, were now not so much to be feared. They are most likely to attack companies beyond Fort Laurimie, and especially those coming from the West, because they say, they have been trading with the Snakes, their enemies. Although it was possible that we might see them between Fort Laurimie and the forks of the Platte, yet, in this part of their country, we knew they were much less to be dreaded: And in addition to this, they were beginning to have a much better idea of the strength of the whites. Formerly they had considered that they were weak, and that their numbers were very small. When the Emigration of 1843 passed through their country, they told the traders at Fort Laurimie, that they believed it to be the white people's big village, and the last of the race. Under this belief, they entertained serious notions, of going back, and taking possession of the country which they had abandoned. But an Emigration of twelve hundred the following year, and one of three thousand the present year, had an effect to open their eyes; and they began to respect their power. Col. Carney's visit this year, with two or three hundred dragoons, had even made them to fear a little, and would, we believed, have a tendency to promote our safety. He had not only passed through the whole extent of their country, as far as the South Pass, but had called together, at Fort Laurimie, as great a number of those tribes as he could; among these were many of their Chiefs and braves, with whom he held a council; not only warning them of the punishment which they would receive, if they continued to molest and kill the Americans, but operating on their superstition, by a display of such things, as to them, were mysterious and supernatural.

After he had had a long talk with the Chiefs, and told them what he wished them to do, and what not to do, in respect to the white people passing through their country, he obtained from them a promise, that they would henceforth, in these respects, act according to his wishes and requests. Having obtained this promise, which without the addition of fear would have been violated as freely as it had been given, he determined to work a little, if possible, upon their superstitions. The dragoons, with all military show, were paraded, and a field piece rolled out upon the prairie. The Colonel then proclaimed to the Chiefs and braves, and to all the Indians assembled, that he was about to inform the Great Spirit of their promise, and call him to witness the covenant which they had made. He bade them look up and listen. A sky-rocket rose in the air, and darting away on its mission, had almost buried itself in the bosom of the sky, when it burst, flashed in the heavens, reported to the Great Mysterious, resolved itself again into its airy form, and the errand was accomplished. Another, and another; three of the firy messengers arose in succession into the presence of the Great Spirit, and announced to him, that the Sioux and Shians had entered into a solemn covenant with a Chief of the white people, to be their friends, and to respect forever their lives and property. While they stood, with all the awe which ignorance and blind superstition could inspire, gazing into the heavens, where, just now they had been luminous with the mysterious display, a cannon was discharged; and while its deafning thunder shook the field, the ball flying, far away along the plain, bounding and rebounding, tore the earth, and marked its dusty track with clouds. "That," said the Colonel, "was to open your ears, that you might not be deaf to what I am about to say. Can you hear?" "Yes," replied the Chiefs, "we can hear." The second was discharged, roaring still louder than the first; and the ball again proved the power of the mighty engine that sent it. "Can you hear, I say?" demanded the Colonel. "Yes," they replied, a little submissively, "we can hear well." Again the cannon told, still louder. Three times it thundered in their ears. "Can you hear?" reiterated the Colonel. "I say, can you hear?" We are not deaf; we can hear well; our ears are open. Speak. Let the great Chief of the white people speak whatever he wishes."

Col. Carney addressed them. "I am," said he, "very little. "The Great Chief of the white people is afar: he is in the bosom "of a mighty nation; and his warriors around him, are like the "grass upon the prairie, or the sands which cover the plains. He "told me to go and talk to the Sioux and Shians, and I obeyed him. "I am here. A thousand Chiefs who are mightier than I, wait to "do his commands. He loves his friends, and is kind to them, but "to his enemies, to those who destroy the lives of his people, he is "dreadful. As the storm when it walks upon the mountains, and "treads down the pines, so terrible are the warriors of the Great "Chief, when they come upon their foes. Beware then, lest ye "make him angry. Think before you break the pipe, which we "have smoked together in friendship. Think well before you vio- "late the covenant you have made with me and with my people, and "to which we have called the Great Spirit to witness. Talk to your "young men; counsel them that are foolish; tell them that "we are mighty, and terrible in war. Bid them pause, and think, "and tremble, before they spill again the blood of a white man. "The past we will forget; it is buried. We will soon return to our "homes, with the tidings of peace: but when we hear that your "hands have spilt one drop more of the blood of our countrymen, "we will come again. We will come with war. We will re- "venge all the wrongs that we have ever received. Then your "eyes shall not be dry from weeping over your fallen warriors, "and the blood of your nations shall not cease to flow, until we "are weary from destroying. You say that you can hear. We "will see. Be careful that your ears do not forget." They all answered, "It is good."

Such, we believe, is about the sense, in which we understood Mr. Bisonette, describing the treaty made by Col. Carney, with the Sioux and Shians. He is one of the principal partners in the neighboring trading establishment, Fort Platte, and we presume that it is mainly correct. He gave us, as his opinion, that for a time, it would have a favorable influence over the conduct of the Indians; but that it would soon be forgotten, and disregarded, and that nothing but a strong military post, located in their country, could keep them in awe, and make the lives of Americans, safe among them.

Our little company, after a short delay, continued down the North Fork. On the 3d of August we approached the spot, where Mr. Adams was remaining, in charge of a large quantity of Buffalo robes, the cargo of one of the boats which had failed in descending the River. He was awaiting the arrival of wagons from Mr. Bisonette, to convey them to the States. As soon as we came in sight of Mr. Adams, we saw a village of Sioux coming, at the same time, from another direction. They arrived a few minutes before us, and were engaged in pitching their lodges when we came up. When we were yet half a mile off, we found two young Indians, sitting beside the road, who rose up, and gave us their hands in token of friendship; and then making signs to us to proceed, they led the way, to where their village was encamping, beside Mr. Adams.

We had been discovered by them from the hills on the South, out of which they came; and the two young men had been dispatched by their Chief, to ascertain our character, and to conduct us, if friends, of which they of course had little doubt, to the village.

Without dismounting, we delivered to Mr. Adams, a letter from Mr. Bisonette; enquired whether we would probably fall in with any of the Sioux below, and whether with the Pawnees; and what, in his opinion, would be their disposition towards us, in case we should. We smoked with the Chief, and after a few minutes conversation with Mr. Adams, from which we could determine nothing satisfactorily, we again turned into the trail, and continued down the river.

The Indians treated us with great civility. They did not crowd around, when we stopped, to pilfer and beg, as Indians generally do about a small party.

When we passed by their encampment, as we were leaving, the

women and children, with some of the young men, came out and stood by the side of the road; and the Chief, and a few of the old men, walked with us three or four hundred yards, in hopes of receiving presents; yet without being importunate. We gave them a little tobacco, and a few other trifles, excusing ourselves for the smallness of our gifts, by telling them that we had traveled very far, and were then poor. They appeared satisfied, gave us their hands and returned.

We encamped a few miles below, and remained about three hours, but none of them came near us. Knowing the disposition of the people we were among, and their uncertainty, we deemed it prudent, however, to make the distance between us greater, before the next morning. But they were the last that we saw of the Sioux Indians; and from what cause they were induced to treat us with so much civility, we are uncertain. We attributed it, at the time, to Col. Carney's treaty with them, and to the imposing display which he exhibited.

Not having provided ourselves very abundantly with meat, while on Sweet Water, and not having seen any game on the North Fork, we began to be fearful, that we should not be able to proçure provisions enough to last us in. But on the 5th of August, crossing over to the South Fork, we found the valley and hills beyond, covered with thousands and thousands of Buffalo. We therefore pitched our camp, on the bank of the river, in the most convenient place we could find, and prepared to "make meat."

On the following morning, two of the best riders and marksmen were selected, and mounted on the strongest and fleetest horses. Having divested themselves of the greater part of their clothing, and whatever else they could spare that would tend to add weight or gather the wind, and being armed with guns and pistols, they proceeded towards the nearest band, which would have numbered, perhaps, about a thousand. They rode along slowly, taking advantage of the wind, until they saw the band begin to notice them: then putting spurs to their horses, they urged the chase at full speed across the plain. Others followed at a less rapid rate, with loose animals, to bring in the meat.

We supposed that some of the largest of these Buffaloes were nearly seven feet high, and would probably weigh more than two thousand pounds.

It was a grand scene to look upon; that vast, living flood, moving on towards the hills, throwing huge clouds of dust into the air, and shaking, with their heavy tread, the very earth. The horsemen gained; and entering the band, which gave way at their approach, and closed around them, they spurred to gain the lead, where the fatest and best Buffalo are always found. Their guns reported rapidly—the herd rushed on. swelling over the alternate hills, until the cloud of dust that marked their course, faded in the distance, and three fine Buffaloes lay stretched along upon the border of the valley. The hunters halted around their prey, butchered it, and the packmen came and bore it to the camp, where we cut it into thin slices, and dried it in the sun; having done which, we again proceeded down the South Fork.

But not being yet sufficiently provided for, we averaged our daily distance of about twenty-five miles, by traveling a large portion of the night; laying by in the middle of the day, when the sun was most powerful, to kill and dry meat. We continued this method of proceedure until we had supplied ourselves with provisions, and then again traveled as usual.

When we came to the junction of the Platte, we found a vast herd of Buffalo, almost covering the valley. They were so thick, that, in many places, they blackened the earth for hundreds of acres. The lowest estimate made in our camp, of the number of that single herd, was, we believe, one hundred thousand, and it was, probably, much greater. During the time that we were passing them, in which we traveled about ten miles, the partially detached or smaller herds extending out from it, became frightened, as we proceeded, and kept pouring across our path, about two hundred yards before us, in an almost constant stream. Besides this, the hills were spotted in every direction, as far as the eye could reach, with bands of Buffalo. Such vast herds are, however, uncommon. Afterwards we ascertained the cause, as we thought, of their being assembled in such vast numbers.

On the morning of the 13th, about two hours before day, while we lay encamped upon the bank of the Grand Platte, we heard a drum beating below us, on the river. We were sure that it was the Pawnees; and, besides, that they were in great numbers, as they were on the middle ground, between their own country and that of the Sioux, where they never come, except in strong parties. We, therefore, made all possible haste to get under way, in order to pass them before they should discover us.

Having traveled a few miles, we passed through a large encampment, which had been left only a very short time; and all along the road, and on every side, there were fresh signs of a large body of Indians; and we had not proceeded much farther, before we were favored with still stronger proofs of it. We saw an Indian gliding along across the prairie, in a direction to meet our course, and then another, and again another, until they were nearly double our number.

They tried in every way to detain us: they endeavored to persuade us to go across to their village, at which, they said, there were fifteen hundred of their people. We refused, and they told us that there were a great many Buffalo a short distance below; that they intended to surround them the next day, and that they did not wish us to go on and frighten them. To this, although we were sure it was false, we replied, that we had an abundance of meat and would not disturb them; and continued still to move on at a rapid rate. They then began to threaten, and finally, finding all of no avail, they rushed out towards the river several hundred yards, and began yelling and throwing up their blankets into the air. In a few minutes after this signal was given, we saw two or three long columns of mounted men emerge from the brush along the bank of the river, and come at full speed towards us. We had but a moment to counsel. Retreat was folly, since it would be impossible for us to gain any shelter, or advantageous place, before they would be on us. To fight, in the open prairie, against such odds—for there were more than forty to one, and would have been supported by four times that number—would have been madness. The only alternative left, was to wait the event, and be ready for the worst. There was a possibility that in this way, by proper management, we might avoid serious difficulty; any other would have been certain destruction. We were, however, determined, of course, to defend our lives and property as best we could, in the last extremity.

Three hundred armed men rushed up and surrounded us. Standing with our backs together, that we might see them draw, and be ready to return the blow, though feebly, when they struck, we watched their tone and movements. They seemed to differ, and to be undecided. Some appeared strongly inclined to insult and abuse; others checking these, seemed to require time to decide. After the expiration of some minutes, an old Indian came up, passed through the crowd, which gave way at his approach, and handed us a folded paper. We read it. It purported to be from the Indian Agent, and was addressed to white people, passing through that country. It stated that this Indian, who called himself White Man, was a Chief of the Pawnees, and had previously saved the lives of a small party from the United States, and returned them their property, which had been taken from them by some of the young men of his tribe; that he was a friend to the white people: and the writer desired those who might meet with him, to make him presents.

This Chief also requested us, to go over with them to the village; telling us the same story which had been told by those who first came to us, that there was a herd of Buffalo below, and that he did not wish us to firighten them away, since he intended to surround them on the following day.

From the character which the paper of the Agent gave the Chief, and from his venerable and friendly appearance, we were now almost persuaded to believe their story about the Buffalo. We hesitated for a moment, and some spoke in favor of going with them to their village. We had never seen Indians making *"a surround,"* and our anxiety urged us strongly. We thought how grand a scene it would be, to see fifteen hundred Pawnees, armed and mounted, after having formed in a circle around a large herd of Buffalo, close in upon them, with whooping, yelling, and firing; and then to see them, after the affrighted herd had scattered, cover the plains afar, with the confused, tumultuous, and excited chase; the whirling clouds of dust; the huge animals that had fallen, laying about on every side; the wild uproar, and the reckless eagerness of the half naked pursuers. Some thought less of looking on, but imagined how glorious it would be, all mounted, armed and flying over the level plain, to mingle in the tumult, pull down the mighty game, and be an Indian for an hour. Had not our homes and friends rose up against this curiosity, and urged us to proceed, we would have gone with the Pawnees to their village, been disappointed in seeing the anticipated sport, and probably, after having been stripped of every thing we had, would have been insulted and abused.

Our desire to hasten on prevailed, and we replied in the same manner as before; told them that we had far to go, and did not wish to delay; and further, that if he was unwilling to trust us, he might send some of his people along, until we had passed the Buffalo, to see that we did not disturb them. He finally consented to this, and we now considered that we were safe. We smoked with the Chief, as a mutual pledge of friendship, made him such presents as our situation and circumstances would afford, and departed, accompanied by twenty-two of his men.

Having gone about ten miles, we halted, and unloaded our animals, that they might eat and rest, as we had been traveling at a rapid rate, from early in the morning until now, which was about the middle of the afternoon.

We expected to part with the Indians here, and therefore openened our bales and offered them something to eat, which they refused to accept, saying they had plenty in their camp. And as soon as our bales were opened, and our baggage scattered, they began taking whatever they could lay their hands on. We saw now that they intended to rob us, and knowing that it would not do to yield to them in the least, we regained what they had taken, with as little force as possible. They feared us, and yielded; but threatened, saying that they would take away every thing we had. We showed them our guns in reply. Hastily reloading our animals, with our arms in our hands, we mounted, pointed them to the backward track, and took the other ourselves.

There was an old Indian who followed us a short distance, and either from friendship, or a desire to learn what course we intended to pursue, told us, with a great pretension of regard for our safety, that "it was good for us not to sleep," but to continue traveling, "after the sun had gone down:" that some of their young men "had bad hearts," and were "very angry;" and that they would follow and attack us in the night. We expressed our thanks for his kindness, without intimating our intentions, and left him.

We had not seen a single Buffalo, nor did we afterwards; and we thought that this was only a scheme they had laid, to get us into the village, where they might strip us more effectually, and without our knowing who did it; and that finding we would not go willingly, they consented to our proposal, thinking that three times our number, would be sufficient to accomplish their object. They probably considered, in addition to this, that by the method which they adopted, the tribe would avoid the responsibility of the act. As the greater portion of those who came to us, had gone away professing friendship, they would, with some degree of probability, have deen able to assert their ignorance, of any intention on the part of those who went with us, to commit a robbery. It was our opinion, that they did not wish to take our lives, if they could obtain our property without; and especially if they could do so by means, in which the tribe would not seem, generally, to participate.

17

Could they have destroyed us entirely, without any possibility of detection, they would have been very willing to have done it; but they had made like attempts severals times before, and failed; they were now a little fearful, for they had been threatened by officers of our government, and had, from experience, some confidence in their ability to execute. Had we gone to their village, they might have stolen almost every thing that we had, and in such case, all would have been innocent. Had the twenty-two succeeded, they only, and not the tribe, would have been criminally responsible. We had no doubt but that all were perfectly acquainted with the intentions of the party that undertook to rob us, and would have been sharers to some extent in the booty; and that, had they considered a failure at all probable, they would have adopted some other surer method of procedure.

The Pawnees were descending the river, and all appearances favored the opinion, that they had been the cause of the great assemblage of Buffalo at the forks of the Platte. Having passed the great band a short distance, very few others were afterwards seen, although the whole valley, on the South side, had been trodden recently, by numerous herds.

That we might not fall into their hands again, we concluded to follow the old Indian's advice; and that we might decieve him also, we determined to do more; and having halted a little before sundown, to take supper and allow our animals to graze, we proceeeded, following the road until it was quite dark, when we left it, and bore off to the South, until we entered the hills: we then turned again, and followed the direction of the river, steering our course by the stars, until after midnight. We then halted and slept till morning without food or water.

As soon as it was light, we again loaded our animals, and steered across the plains for the waters of the Kanzas, which we thought we could reach in a day's travel.

About 12 o'clock we began to differ about the course we were traveling, and came near separating, but finally agreed by changing it a little; and in the evening, after having traveled about forty miles, we came to a tree, by a small brake that ran towards the the East, in which we found a pool of water, and stopped for the night.

The way across, between the Platte and the waters of the Kanzas, before the emigrants had made a beaten track, had always been considered very difficult to find. The distance at different places, varies between twenty five and fifty miles; the country is level and monotonous, and has not a single land-mark, by which the traveler may be guided. Many persons much more experienced on *the prairie* than we, had been lost in attempting to pass from one stream to the other; and the country, from this circumstance, had obtained the name of "The Lost Ground." The Catholic Priest, who was still with us, being a foreigner, and not at all accustomed to moving at random, without track or guide, through such wilds, became alarmed at our situation, and declared he was certain that we should never find the trail, and he would be very glad, he said, to give every thing he possessed, to see again the track of a wagon. We were fortunate in changing our course, for if we had not done so, we should have missed entirely, the head of Little Blue River, and would have been compelled to travel another day, and perhaps longer, before we would have come to another stream.

This fortunate circumstance--finding the pool--was highly pleasing to us. It had been nearly twenty-four hours since we had drunk water, and we had been traveling rapidly during the day, over the dry plains and through the hot sun. We noticed, in the course of the day, that our voices became much changed, from lack of moisture, and as we refrained from eating, also, there was a feeling of emptiness in the stomach, peculiar, and very disagreeable. When we came to the pool, our parched lips did not stop to question the quality of the water: and our animals were equally as eager as ourselves: they plunged into it, and we were compelled to drag them away to prevent them from killing themselves. The person whose turn it was to guard during the day, was obliged to watch the pool almost constantly, in order to keep the animals from drinking too much. We climbed into the tree with our hatchets, and trimmed off the dry limbs, which furnished us sufficient fuel to cook with; and in a very short time, we had banished both hunger and thirst, and feeling secure in our secluded and unfrequented position, we contrasted this present comparatively comfortable and safe condition, very pleasantly with the past.

In the morning we followed the breaks until they joined with others, and finally brought us to a deep dry channel, along which there was timber; it continued to increase in size; as we proceeded down, and on the 16th of August, about the middle of the day we came again to the emigrant's trail, and knew that it was the Little Blue River, down which we had been traveling.

We saw no more of the Pawnees, and on the 22d we crossed the

Big Blue River, and came into the country of the Kanzas Indians, from whom we had nothing to fear so long as we kept a strict guard; which we never failed to do in an Indian country.

On the 24th, we met a small company bound for California, and on the 25th, the wagons of Messrs. Adams & Bissonette, Indian traders, of Fort Platte.

On the 27th, we crossed the Kanzas River; where, finding the water too deep to take our baggage on our horses, we were compelled to carry it over on our shoulders.

On the 29th, late in the night, we passed the boundary line, between the States and the Indian Territory, and encamped near West Post, Missouri, having become lost and bewildered among the roads and fences, to which we were unaccustomed. The darkness of night hid every mark of civilization when we came; and we slept, without appreciating the change. We awoke with the rising sun, to look upon fields, orchards, gardens, houses and villages; our country and our countrymen.

NOTE.—By a little inadvertency this Chapter was numbered the same as the preceding one; it will be perceived that it should be VII.

CHAPTER VIII.

GENERAL VIEW OF OREGON AND CALIFORNIA.

Concluding remarks, giving a brief but general view of Oregon and California as regards the Agricultural, Manufacturing, and Commercial advantages of those countries, &c., &c.

As we have now completed our explorations in both Oregon and California, we will make a few remarks upon their fitness for the occupancy, and various uses of civilized man.

As we have already said, the climate, in Oregon and California, is far milder and more agreeable, than it is in the same parallel of latitude, any where on the Eastern side of the American continent. There is, we think, a difference of perhaps 10 or 12 deg. We suppose that some may think this difference too great, but when they recollect that animals can live well through the winter, in Oregon, in the 47th deg. of North latitude, and that scarcely any snow falls during this season of the year; and that that which does fall, even in this high latitude, lays but a very short time, in the lower and more productive valleys; and that good beef is often killed in mid-winter from the grass, any where between the Cascade Mountains and the Pacific Ocean, South of the Columbia River; and then recollect what the Winters are in the United States, even as far South as the 25th deg. North, we are inclined to believe, that most, if not all, will be ready to believe, that we are nearly correct in regard to this matter.

As the farmer's stock can live well all winter, not only throughout California, but through nearly the whole of Oregon, he will here possess one advantage that he can never have East of the Rocky Mountains, except in the most Southern part of the United States; consequently, he will not be compelled, as he is in most parts of the great and fertile Valley of the Mississippi, to labor six months to produce grain and provender, to feed out, at the expense of another six months' labor, to his stock. And there is not only in the territory of Oregon, but also in the province of California, another great advantage, that is, indeed, paramount to all others;

which is, health. Those countries, with the exception of a few small localities, are, beyond all doubt, and must ever remain, very healthy. Some of the causes which make them so, must be obvious to all, who become acquainted with those countries. They are high, dry, rolling, mountainous, and well watered with the purest springs and streams; and come the wind from whatever point it may, it must ever be free from miasma and disease, as it always comes, either from snow clad mountains or passes over the pure and untainted waves of the briny Ocean.

There is, however, one drawback to the mild, and otherwise pleasant winters, over a large portion of the countries we have seen and discribed; on the western shores of our continent: which is, the great amount of dark, cloudy, and rainy weather, through most of the winter season. The rains, however, as it has already been seen, do not generally fall in heavy showers, but are, mostly, gentle and light, and often, nothing more than heavy mist. We are inclined to believe, that little if any more water falls there, in the winter, than falls in most parts of the Mississtppi Valley; with this difference, that there it is rain instead of snow.

In those countries, as in the Mississippi Valley, the winters do, in some degree, vary. When compared with the winters East of the Rocky Mountains, they are always mild; yet some are more so than others, and some are much dryer than others. The first winter we passed, West of the mountains, was milder, dryer, and much more agreeable than the second; indeed, there was much of the first that was dry, sunny, and agreeable, beyond anything we had ever before witnessed. The second was more rainy and disagreeable. But as far South as the Bay of San Francisco, in California, it is never colder, even in the winter, than to produce heavy white frost.

We believe that small grains of every description, that are raised in the United States, will grow well, and produce abundantly, throughout Oregon, and over all the Upper or Northern portion of California. So also, will the grasses; but Indian Corn never will, as the nights are too cool in Summer, over all those regions, for the thrifty growth and proper ripening of this grain; it can, however, be raised in small quantities, but the farmer there, can never grow it to much profit.

The Willammette Valley is, perhaps, the largest district of productive country in Oregon. Something more than two thirds of it is open, or prairie land, and the largest part of this is rich; the prairies, indeed, generally, through the country, when turned up by the plow, make very much the same black, rich appearance, they mostly bear in the Mississippi Valley; some doubt, however, their being as durable, as there seems to be a great absence of lime. Near one third of this valley is timbered, and the timber is mostly good, and as it furnishes great manufacturing, as well as agricultural privileges, it would be capable of sustaining, were every portion of it made to yield to the best advantage, a population of nearly a million of souls.

The Umqua Valley is, perhaps, three-fourths prairie. The Rogue's River Valley, two-thirds, and the Clamuth, four fifths.

In many places through these several valleys, the prairies are of convenient size to be entirely settled and cultivated; in others they are so large that it will be inconvenient; but as the neighboring mountain lands, are, with few exceptions, thickly clothed with the finest timber in the world, they will, in time, all be brought into cultivation.

North of the Columbia, and West of he Cascade Mountains, there is, perhaps, not more than one third of the country that is not timbered, and much of it stands so thick on the ground, is so tall and large, that it will not only make lumber most abundant in the country, but it must long, if not always, be capable of furnishing immense quantities for exportation.

The valleys, through this portion of Oregon, are smaller than they are, South of the river; here the country has more broken, mountain, waste land, and consequently it cannot sustain so large a population. It is thought, that considerable portions of the timbered land between the Cascade Mountains and the Pacific, both North and South of the Columbia, is good for cultivation, though mostly, if not always, much inferior in point of productiveness, to the prairie lands.

The Cawlitz Valley, North of the Columbia, like the Willammette, South, furnishes, perhaps, the largest valley of land, suitable for cultivation, between the Cascades and the Ocean; but on the North, as well as the South side, there are many other smaller valleys, besides these, capable of sustaining considerable settlements; which will, altogether, in time, when all that can, is made to yield, furnish agricultural products, sufficient to sustain a population of some millions.

And through this whole region of country, many of the hills

and mountains, will furnish the best, and healthiest pastures for sheep; and there cannot be a doubt, but that hundreds of thousands of these useful animals, can be kept in the finest condition, between the Cascade Mountains and the Pacific; to furnish the factories that are destined to rise up at no far distant day, in this great world of water power, with heavy fleeces of the finest wool.

Should the United States maintain her claim to the entire Territory of Oregon, she will then have Puget's Sound, the second best Harbor on the Western shores of America, and a considerable district of country around it, said to be good; besides the whole of Vancouver's Island, which, of itself, is capable of sustaining a considerable colony; but as it is most likely that the 49th parallel of latitude will be the boundary settled upon, as the Northern limit of our territory, it is doubtful whether we will possess the fine Harbor of Puget's Sound, and we shall not have more than one third of Vancouver's Island.

The country East of the Cascade Mountains, and laying between them and the Blue Mountains, is an excellent grazing country. Immediately on the streams, and along the base of the mountains, there are many narrow strips of fertile land, suitable for cultivation, and these portions of rich soil, though small when compared with the entire country containing them, (not more, we think, than one tenth part,) will probably be enongh to grow a sufficiency of agricultural products, to sustain a large grazing population. And that this country will, at some future day, be filled with such a population, there cannot be a doubt; as it contains, in most places over all the country known as a the Walawala Valley, an abundance of the most nutritious grass, so that, within the bounds of this valley, great numbers of stock can be kept through the year; and although the valley contains no timber, with the exception of Cotton Wood along some of the streams, as the neighboring mountains are mostly well timbered, and as a large portion of the tilable land lies immediately along the base of the mountains, and convenient to the timber, most of the farms could be furnished with it very readily. But those that might be improved on the streams, would, most of them, have to be furnished with the necessary timber, at the expense of much labor, as it could only be had from the mountains, at a distance, in some places, of many miles.

Inasmuch as there is a river called Walawala, some might suppose the valley bearing the name, to be the valley of that stream, and that, therefore, the manner in which we have spoken of it is incorrect; but upon noticing particularly our description, and finding that not only the Walawala, the Snake River, and many other smaller streams, but that the great Columbia itself, runs through it, they will at once see that the valley has not obtained its name from the river, but that the name applies to a portion of country bounded by high mountains, both on the East and West, and stretches North and South some three hundred miles, covering an area equal to twelve or fifteen thousand square miles. This large district of country is not only good for raising and keeping horses, mules, and cattle, but it will be very good for sheep also, as great numbers of them can be raised and kept in the finest and healthiest condition.

This valley has, also, much water power.

The Blue Mountains, which form the Eastern boundary of the Walawala Valley, cover an extent of country about seventy-five miles broad, and are, we believe, about nine-tenths timbered; through these mountains there are numerous small valleys, furnishing in many places, good soil, and every where fine pasture, upon which stock of every description can be kept in good condition throughout the year. But as the valleys in the mountains do not, perhaps, cover more than one twentieth of the whole area, this portion of country could only sustain a sparse population, and keep a limited amount of stock.

The entire country East of the Blue Mountains, including the Rocky Mountains and a broad belt of country some five hundred miles wide, East of them, embracing altogether a tract of some one thousand or eleven hundred miles broad, is, with the exception of some small spots—widely, very widely separated from each other, a vast and dreary desert—a sandy, dusty, rocky waste. Over much of this desert region, there are large dusty tracts, on which there is almost no vegetation. These dusty regions bear much the appearance of ashes and burnt earth, mixed.

The small spots of productive soil that are scattered over this great desert of America, cannot amount to much if any more than one thousandth part of the whole. From which it will be seen, that it is better calculated to sustain small bands of savages living after the manner of the wandering Arabs, than any fixed population of agriculturalists.

South of the Snowy Butte, which is not far from the parallel of

42 deg. North, to the head of the Sacramento Valley, a distance of one hundred miles, the country is entirely covered with timber. It is mountainous, and contains no land fit for cultivation; and although much of the timber in these mountain regions is of excellent quality, it is so far removed from the extensive plains of California, laying far South, that it can never be taken to them to make enclosures for farms; and much of the country where it grows, is so exceedingly broken, that it will be difficult to take it out for any purpose. But from many parts of this extensive tract of timber, immense quantities can and will be taken out in lumber for all purposes, and used in many distant parts of the province; and by way of the Sacramento, it may be taken into the Bay of San Francisco, and from the thence wherever wanted.

The Sacramento Valley, which probably contains about ten thousand square miles, is nearly or quite, one-third timbered and one-half suitable for cultivation. Much of the soil is very fertile.

From the Bay of Francisco to Monte Rey, and between the California Mountains and the Coast, including the Valley of St. Wakine, covering an area of near twenty thousand square miles, there is not more than one-tenth of the country timbered; but nearly one half is fit for tillage, with some very pooductive lands.

From Monte Rey to the Lower Puebla, embracing the Southern portion of Northern or Upper California, there is, perhaps, not more than one-hundredth part of the land timbered, and one-twentieth, suitable for cultivation; but there is a much greater portion good for grazing.

The Sacramento and St. Wakine Valleys, furnish much the largest body of good country in California. Indeed from the health of this country, which is good beyond all doubt; from the great mildness of the climate; the fertility of much of its soil, and the great commercial advantages it will have, by means of the noble Bay of San Francisco; it must, at no distant day, become a very desirable, if not the most desirable country on the Continent.

When it is recollected, as we have heretofore stated, that over a large portion of Upper California, fresh meat will keep good, hung in the open air, at any season of the year, for several days together, without salt; there can be no doubt of the great purity of the atmosphere, and consequent health of the country.

Most of the Northern portion of the Province has a sufficiency of good water power; but in the South, the supply is less abundant: and in some parts, it is very deficient.

When this Province shall have been settled, by an industrious and enterprising population, disposed to avail themselves of all the advantages which Nature has so bountifully spread out, over this country; it will be covered with vast multitudes of stock of all kinds; the upper country will become a manufacturing district, and every where, on and around the extensive Bay of San Francisco, the most active and extensive commercial operations will be constantly going on.

But no country of which we have any knowledge, is so fitted by nature to become one great manufacturing region, as the territory of Oregon. It has every where, over it, an abundance of never failing water power, sufficient to propel machinery of any kind and to any amount; and as we have already said, all parts of the territory are suitable for raising the finest sheep, (not excepting the be s ever reared in Spain,) and over this country sufficient numbers can and will be raised, to keep the numerous and extensive factories in constant operation.

But little is yet known of the minerals of the country. Some lead and iron have been discovered; and if an intimate acquaintance with the country shall discover an abundance of the metals, then will there be nothing wanting, to make Oregon one of the greatest manufacturing countries in the world, but the necessary population and capital; both of which, time and the enterprise of our countrymen, will give. And, although much of it is rocky and mountainous, and every where over it, are strong and evident marks of powerful, and not very remote volcanic action; as the country is very healthy, the climate mild, and the volcanoes, from appearances, mostly, if not all except Mount St. Helen, extinct; we think the day not distant, when it will be sufficiently peopled to carry on extensive manufacturing and commercial operations. And as it is situated for carrying on a direct trade with the South Sea Islands, all the countries on the Western shores of South America, and with China, the trade of which, under the treaties that have been made with this country, since the British war, must, in a few years, be extensive and important, Oregon must, at some future day, become a great Commercial as well as Manufacturing country.

But we do not profess to give a full description of these countries. There is no one whose knowledge concerning them is not very limited. After the natives, from whom, of course, little is to be learned, those who have longest inhabited them, and traveled over them most, the traders, are nearly all illiterate; and the few who were somewhat competent to investigate and judge, have had their minds wholly engrossed with other matters. A few years is insufficient to acquire a particular knowledge of such extensive territories. It yet remains for others to explore, discover, and make known, many of the hidden resources and subjects of interest, with which those remote, new, and peculiar regions, most probably abound,

APPENDIX.

INSTRUCTIONS TO EMIGRANTS—SUPPLIES AND EQUIPMENT—MANNER OF TRAVELING, &c.—BILL OF THE ROUTE.

The distance from the Western Settlements of the United States to the Settlements in Oregon or California, is variously estimated from twenty-two to twenty-five hundred miles; and the kind of country through which emigrants have to pass, will be seen from the foregoing description; it will also be perceived, that there is but a small portion of this country in which they can supply themselves with provisions. Nothing can be obtained at the trading establishments, except at an enormous price; and the Buffalo are not to be depended on. Under these circumstances, it is of the first importance, that emigrants furnish themselves amply with provisions, before they leave the United States. It requires about five months to make the journey, under ordinary circumstances; but difficulties and detentions may, in some instances, increase the time to six months; it will therefore be the safest, and most prudent, for emigrants to lay in provisions for six months. In respect to the quantity, every one should make a calculation, and judge, partially at least, for himself. In making such a calculation, it is important to take into consideration, the fact, that the appetite is almost universally increased by traveling. It is peculiarly so on the way across the Rocky Mountains. The rough manner of living, which it is necessary for the traveler to adopt, together with the purity of the atmosphere, the constant and wholesome exercise, and the various scenes and incidents daily presented, which tend to divert the mind, all have a great tendency to promote uncommon good health, and consequently, uncommon good appetites. For this reason, it will be found easy to dispense with most of the mere luxuries common to civilized life. With but few exceptions it is only those things which are the most substantial and nutritious that should be taken; such as flour, middlings of bacon, because they are free from bones, rice, sugar, coffee, salt, pepper, &c. The quantity of flour for each individual, should not be less than two huudred pounds, unless the company be entirely made up of pack-men, who intend to make the journey in as short a time as practicable. Where a company carries their provisions, packed on mules, they can generally make the trip about a month sooner, than those who go with wagons can, and therefore the quantity of provisions should be proportionately reduced; one hundred and fifty pounds of flour will be an abundant supply for a packman. Other articles of provision should be taken in the same proportion with the flour, excepting meat, which should be something less. The quantity of meat should be such, that it could be made to last conveniently, five months. There is scarcely ever a year, in which emigrants will not be able to kill some game between the point where they first come to the Platte River and the summit of the Rocky Mountains, and by taking sufficient meat with them from the States *to do*, by stinting themselves a little, they may expect to obtain enough from the Buffalo to complete an abundant supply, but beyond this they should not trust to the fortune of the hunter.

From the moment in which emigrants leave the Western settlements, they should be exceedingly careful of every morsel that may be used with propriety for the support of life. Persons who have been always accustomed to the overflowing abundance of food so bountifully bestowed by Providence upon our country, are very apt to be a little careless in this particular. They are almost sure to acquire habits of wastefuless, which, though they be of little consequence in a land of plenty, if they be not laid aside on *the prairie*, may cause the traveler to look back repentingly, upon the numerous littles which have been daily thrown away, and which, had they been saved, would have prevented the want consequent upon such neglect. Atoms make Mountains; and a little daily waste, in the course of five or six months, will amount to something very considerable in the eyes of a hungry man, when he is surrounded by a desert country where no food can be obtained.

It will be necessary, of course, for families to have wagons, and little companies of three or four young men, will generally find it more comfortable and convenient to travel in that manner. Every thing can be carried with far more ease and less exposure, than on the backs of mules; neither are the things carried so liable to accident. After the provisions, the means of conveyance, wagons, teams, &c., are of the next importance. Wagons should be selected with the greatest care; those should be taken which are made out of the best material, well put together, and properly proportioned. The irons on the wheels should be as tight as possible, without breaking or straining the wood; and the whole wagon should only be heavy enough to bare the required load. It is necessary to have the tires tight on the wheels, on account of the hot dust and sand through which they have to go, and which is very liable to loosen them from the wood.

It will also be well for those who wish to be provided against every circumstance that is liable to come in the way, to construct the beds of their wagons in such a manner that they can be corked and converted into boats. It matters not about the shape; and as they will be used every day as wagon beds, and perhaps never as boats, they had better retain the shape of the former. The covering of the wagon should be of strong and very close material, or painted so as to render it impervious to the heavy rains, which are likely to be encountered on the waters of the Kanzas, and on the Platte.

The kind of teams taken upon this road, is also a matter to which the emigrant should pay very great attention. In an outfit, it is one of the things second in importance: after the provisions, probably the first: for if a team fails, it will be very difficult to replace it. The emigrant is entirely dependant on his team; because if it be not sound, healthy and strong, it will not be able to keep pace with those that are, and he will, in consequence, be forced to some disadvantageous extremity, to avoid falling behind. It will be wise to provide against such accidental circumstances, by taking along extra animals.

Taking every thing into consideration, oxen are preferable to any other animals, for teams. It is true they cannot endure the heat, the want of sufficient food, and other hardships incident to the journey, quite so well as mules; neither can they travel with the same speed: but with moderate traveling, and propper care, they will make the trip, and may be kept in good traveling condition. They are the kind of teams generally used, and are not likely to be stolen by the Indians; and, in addition, they are more serviceable to a farmer improving in a new country; and, in Oregon, they are more valuable, in proportion to the cost in the States, than either mules or horses. All animals that are expected to do service on the road, should be of mature age. A mule should not be less than five years old, and a horse not less than seven. Oxen should also be rather light, and not very large; because this kind are found to travel better than others that are different. If horses are taken with the expectation of having them to do constant service, the Indian horses had better be obtained, if possible; for there are but very few horses that have been raised in the United States, that will not fail to reach the settlements in Oregon or California, if constant service is required of them.

The greatest attention should be paid to all animals that are taken on this journey: they should never be made to perform any work that is not absolutely necessary, and they should always have water and grass when they require it, if it can possibly be obtained. It will be well to stop once in every few weeks, where a good pasture is found, in order to rest the teams. Neither wagons nor teams should be overloaded, for it is bad for either to fail, on the prairie. And there is another thing in connection with this, that ought to be avoided. Many persons preparing to emigrate, who have been unable to sell their little property, have crowded all sorts of trumpery into their wagons, to be hauled to Oregon. This is generally thrown away when it has been hauled six or seven hundred miles, and after it has broken down either the wagon or the team. Persons should remember, that the distance from their starting point to that of their destination, is from twenty-five hundred to three thousand miles; which is rather a long land carriage, especially where the articles taken are of little value. Almost every article which is indispensable to persons wishing to engage in any ordinary occupation, may be had in Oregon, at a very reasonable rate; and in California, for far less than what it will be worth to haul it three thousand miles, across the Rocky Mountains.

Every family should be provided with a commodious tent, made of some kind of strong, close, cotton cloth. It will be found to add much to the comfort of traveling, both as a protection against the sun and rain. A tent also affords a convenient sleeping place, and one in which families may enjoy the privilege of being somewhat to themselves.

Cooking utensils should be such as are in character with a camp; light, simple, and not liable to be broken.

Emigrants should be provided with a good supply of strong and durable clothing; enough to last seven or eight months, or until they can arrive at their destination, and have convenient time to procure others. But this is sufficient; more is worse than superfluous, especially for those who intend going to Oregon. In Oregon, articles of clothing may be obtained at about as reasonable rates as they generally are in new countries, and very much cheaper than they can be carried in wagons, over land, from the United States. It will be proper to take a few articles suitable for Indian trade; such as colored shirts and blankets, butcher-knives, awls, tobacco, beads, vermillion, &c.; for the Indians often have things, which the emigrant would be glad to obtain. A very small supply of such things will, however, be sufficient.

If a number of persons would join, or if a single individual wished to be furnished with goods, tools, implements of husbandry, or any thing else, in Oregon, to a considerable amount, they might be had there more certainly, and for a much less price, by purchasing them, or having them purchased, in some of the Eastern Cities, and having them shipped around the Horn.

Every male person who is of sufficient age to bear arms, should be provided with a gun, and a good supply of ammunition. The kind of guns which are preferable for such a trip, are large and strong rifles: their balls should not be less than one fiftieth of a pound, and they would be better if they were larger. The stock, which is very liable to be broken, should be made uncommonly strong at the brtich, and all parts of the piece which are liable to wear or break, should be effectually tried before leaving the settlements. This is also a matter which should not be disregarded. It is necessary to be properly armed, to insure safety; those who are not, have no business in an Indian country. Five pounds of powder will be an abundant supply for those who intend to hunt a great deal; for those who do not intend to hunt much, half that quantity will probably be sufficient. The amount of lead, it will be remembered, should be four times that of the power. Emigrants generally supply themselves over-abundantly with these articles.

It will be impossible for great numbers to travel together in the same company. It is necessary that the companies should be as small as will be consistant with their safety, in order that they may not be so much delayed in traveling, and that the animals of the several companies may be supplied with grass. It will not be difficult for any one to imagine how delays will occur, where a great number of wagons are traveling together. And grass is found in many places, in quantities sufficient for small companies, but not for large ones.

One hundred men well armed, may travel in safety, by conducting themselves properly, through the most dangerous part of the country, that is, the country laying between Big Blue River, one of the main branches of the Kanzas River, and Green River, of the Gulf of California, which is to be crossed, a few day's travel beyond the summit of the Rocky Mountains. From Green River to the settlements in Oregon, fifty men will make a company sufficiently strong, to avoid or repel all danger.

The character of the Indians will be learned from our preceding remarks. The manner in which they are treated, will, of course, make a great difference in their disposition towards those who chance to meet with them. They should never be trusted, nor should they, if it can be avoided, be allowed to have the advantage in any particular. And while every thing that would be calculated to give them offence, should be carefully avoided by those who wish to go in peace, they should at the same time, be constantly held at a distance. The emigrant should refrain from all familiarity himself, and discourage it in them. In trading with them he should make use of few words; never attempt to deceive, and be prompt to the letter, in fulfilling every promise. Few presents should be given them, and those few should appear to be given, rather as an expression of friendship, than to concilitate their favor. Under all circumstances, the least expression of fear should be sternly avoided. From the late difficulties with the Shoshonee Diggers, and with the Walawalas—to which we have referred—these tribes will not likely be well disposed towards emigrants. Previously, those who have gone into Oregon, have become, after traveling thus far, impatient and careless; have separated into very small companies, and poorly armed, have hastened on, regarding nothing but the termination of the journey. What these have been compelled to submit to and endure, should be a warning to others. Companies passing through these tribes should consist of not less than thirty, well armed men.

The time of leaving the United States, will vary with the season. Companies should start as soon as the grass will admit, which will vary from the latter part of April, through the month of May. The road is so well marked that there will be no difficulty in finding it, and a pilot would only be useful, to direct the manner of traveling, &c., and to point out the best places for encampment. For the benefit of those who wish to emigrate to Oregon, we subjoin a bill of the route.

BILL OF THE ROUTE.

	Miles.	Total.	
From INDEPENDENCE to Crossing of the Kanzas,	90		This is the general estimate of the distance, to the point where emigrants usually cross this river. At the season in which companies for Oregon or California generally leave the States, there is, in this distance, every where, an abundance of wood, water, and grass. The Kanzas River is generally full in the Spring, but emigrants will probably hereafter be accommodated, by a Frenchman who resides at the crossing place, with a ferry-boat. Owing to the time required in crossing, and the consequent accumulation of great numbers of animals, the grass in this vicinity, will likely become, in a few days, insufficient.
Muddy Creek, -	17	107	From the crossing, the road leaves the river gradually to the left. Here there is an abundance of wood and grass. The creek is small but deep, and the crossing has formerly been difficult.
Honey Creek, -	20	127	In the intermediate distance, the road, which still continues to leave the Kanzas River more and more to the left, crosses, every few miles, small creeks upon which there are good camps. At Honey Creek, there is the greatest abundance of wood and grass.
A small creek -	9	136	Upon this, there is much grass—some wood.
Another, - -	3	139	do do
Another, - -	4	143	do do
Canon-Ball Creek, -	2	145	Upon Cannon-Ball Creek, there is an abundance of grass and wood.
A branch, - -	11	156	But little wood—grass abundant.
Another, - -	5	161	do do
Another, - -	3	164	do do
Vermillion, - -	2	166	This is a large creek, and near it there is wood and grass in she greatest abundance.
A small creek, -	12	178	Grass and wood are abundant.
Another, - -	5	183	do do
Big Blue, - -	3	186	This is a river of considerable size, and at this season of the year it is frequently high and difficult to cross; but its bottom lands are covered with timber, which serves to make rafts, or canoes, and in the vicinity there is a great deal of grass.
Battle Creek, -	11	197	At Battle Creek, the grass is abundant, and the quantity of wood is sufficient for camps.
A small creek, -	9	206	Grass abundant. Wood.
Another, - -	15	221	do do
Another, - -	8	229	do do
Another, - -	14	243	do do
Another, - -	10	253	do do
Another, - -	7	260	do do
Little Blue, - -	5	265	The small streams intermediate between Battle Creek and the Little Blue River, in the

	Miles.	Total.	
			Autumn, frequently cease to flow; but in the Spring they generally afford a sufficient quantity of water, wood, and grass, for camps.
To the point where the road leaves Little Blue, - -	51	316	Where the trail follows Little Blue River, there is found, all along, an abundance of wood and grass. Thus far the road passes through a country, much the largest portion of which is fertile; affording every where, grass sufficient to supply the animals of the largest Emigration; neithor—as will be seen by the foregoing notes—will water or wood be wanting. Thus far, there will be no difficulty on account of the uneveness of the surface of the country, but the rains which are here frequent, during that portion of the year in which emigrants will be passing through it, will generally occasion delay; will sometimes render the streams impassable for several days, and where large companies are traveling together, or several smaller ones near each other, the road, in such instances, will of course, become muddy.
The Great Platte, -	25	341	Water is not found in this distance, and the trail, after leaving Little Blue, bears very much to the North until it strikes the Platte—sometimes called the Nebraska.
The Forks, - -	99	440	From the point where the road strikes the river to the union of the North and South branches, there is, in most places a sufficiency of grass on the bottom land, through which the trail passes, seldom leaving the stream more than two or three miles. Wood is seldom found here, though in its absence, a substitute can be obtained which the emigrant will soon become acquainted with. There is wood on some of the islands in the river. At the Forks there is a very large timbered island, and a few trees along on the main shore.
Crossing of South Fork,	71	511	The trail, in this distance, follows near the South bank of the South Fork. On this branch there is not so much grass as there is on the main river, but what there is, is rich, and animals need not suffer. Very little wood. The manner of crossing, in case the stream is high, has been described.
To the North Fork,	15	526	From the South Fork, the trail bears again very much to the North and crosses the high dividing land between the two branches, and descends into Ash Hollow, on the opposite side. There is no wood in this distance, and no water, except some standing in pools, which is very bad. In Ash Hollow there is excellent wood, grass, and water. The mouth of Ash Hollow is within a few hundred yards of the North Fork, and the trail, from this point, with one exception, follows the stream to Fort Laramie. The grass is not so abundant on this, as

	Miles.	Total.	
			on the South Fork, but it will be found sufficient, generally, for the accommodation of companies. A few small cedar trees will be found on the bluffs, for some miles above the mouth of Ash Hollow, but with this exception, there is no wood to be found, worthy of notice, between this point and Scott's Bluffs. As the trail never leaves the river far, water may be always had by going off from it a short distance.
A rich bottom, -	7	533	This spot will afford grass sufficient for several large companies.
A small creek, -	30	563	
Another, - -	2	565	
A large creek, -	10	575	
The Chimney, -	20	595	The trail leaves the river, a few miles beyond the Chimney.
Scott's Bluffs. -	20	615	On the East side of Scott's Bluffs, where the trail passess over them, there is a large spring of excellent water, an abundance of wood, and grass enough for two or three large companies.
Horse creek, -	12	627	In the intermediate distance, there is neither water nor grass. At Horse Creek there is an abundance of grass and rushes, but scarcely any wood.
North Fork, -	15	642	An abundance of grass and wood.
Fort Laramie, -	20	662	The trail, in this distance, follows the river; along which the bottoms are wooded; affording always plenty of fuel, and generally ample pasturage. At Fort Laramie, the trail crosses Laramie Fork, a small river which is sometimes too deep to ford; but if it should be, meens can probably be obtained at the Fort to ferry it. There is generally but little grass here, and it will be prudent for companies to delay no longer than necessity absolutely requires. Wood, in this vicinity, is almost entirely wanting.
Warm Springs, -	11	673	Between Fort Larimie and this point, there is no water, without descending to the North Fork, which will be very difficult. At the Warm Springs, there is an abundance of wood, and there will be no difficulty in using the water; but the grass is sufficient only for a few small companies. They are a few hundred yards to the right of trail. These Springs are at the entrance of the Black Hills, and the road beyond them, is, in many places, steep and rocky; but from the last waters of the Kanzas, thus far, it is certainly an excellent one.
A small creek, -	8	681	Wood. Grass abundant, on the hills.
A large creek, -	20	701	In the intermediate distance, there are several small streams which are dry in the latter part of Summer, but in the season in which emigrants pass, water will be found every few miles; an abundance of wood, and grass sufficient for camps.
North Fork, -	5	706	On the river at this place, there is plenty of

	Miles.	Total.	
			wood and grass. Here there are two roads, one following the river, and the other leaving it to the right. That will be preferable which has been least traveled, on account of grass.
The North Fork, -	55	761	This is by the road which leaves the river. Through the Black Hills, there are, in the Spring season, numerous small streams which afford water, a great deal of wood, and grass sufficient for several companies. In this distance, the streams are never more than six miles apart.
The crossing, -	30	791	From the point where the two roads again unite, the trail follows the North Fork to the crossing, never leaving it far. In the bottoms of the stream, there is grass sufficient for camps, and an inexhaustable quantity of wood. The River here, at this season, can generally be forded. If it be high, recourse must be had to rafting, unless emigrants are otherwise provided. Timber is not wanting.
Water,	16	807	Immediately after crossing the Platte, the trail leaves the river entirely, and bears to the right, over a high and uneven country, which affords very little of either wood, water, or grass; and until it reaches Sweet Water, a small river tributary to the North Fork, the most of the water is impregnated with some kind of salts, which render it worse than disagreeable. At this place, there is a spring, and a channel, in which the water sometimes flows. Water salt. Grass scarce. No wood.
Salt Sink, -	10	817	Here, immediately on the trail, the water is salt, and there is scarcely any grass; but green spots may be seen to the right among the hills, where there is excellent grass, and springs of good water. They are five or six hundred yards from the road. Great caution must be observed, to keep out of the sinks, which are numerous, dangerous, and deceptive. No wood.
Willow Springs, -	7	824	Excellent water, some willow brush, and good grass, for a few companies.
Large marsh,	2	826	Water and grass for a few companies. No wood. A small branch flows from this marsh, along which there is some grass. The trail follows it a few miles.
Crooked creek, -	11	837	But little grass, and no wood.
Independence Rock,	8	845	This is on the bank of Sweet Water, along which there is good grass, but not much wood.
Grand Pass, -	97	942	This is to some large and excellent springs, a few miles beyond the head of Sweet Water, and near the summit of the Pass through the Rocky Mountains, (South Pass.) From the Independence Rock, the trail follows Sweet Water, never leaving it far, to its source. In most places, the bottoms along the stream are cov-

	Miles.		
		Total.	
			ered with an abundance of excellent grass. There is very little wood. At the springs in the Pass, grass is abundant, but wood is entirely wanting.
Water, - -	10	952	Water salt. Little grass. No wood.
Little Sandy, -	9	961	A creek—very good grass, and some wood—trail crosses the stream, and follows down six miles.
Big Sandy, - -	12	973	Grass, and some wood—trail crosses—trail follows the course of the stream, but leaves it some distance to the left.
Big Sandy, - -	18	991	The same stream. Grass and wood.
Green River, -	6	997	A large stream which is often too deep to ford, but there is plenty of timber on its banks, out of which to construct rafts, if it should be necessary. Grass is abundant. After crossing the river, the trail follows it down 12 miles.
Green River, -	12	1009	Wood plenty. Grass scarce.
Ham's Fork, -	18	1027	Trail crosses. Good grass. Wood plenty.
Black's Fork, -	1	1028	
A trading house, -	28	1056	Establishment of Bridgers and Vasques, situated on Black's Fork. In the intermediate distance, the trail follows the stream, along which there are good places for encampments. Near the Trading House, both grass and wood are very abundant.
Bear River, -	70	1126	From the trading post, the trail follows a branch of Black's Fork to its source, passes over a short dividing ridge, to the head of a small branch, which it follows down to Bear river. Grass and wood are scarce.
Soda Springs, -	80	1206	These springs are on Bear river. In the intermediate distance, the trail runs down the valley of the stream, which is mostly covered with excellent grass. Wood is scarce. At the Soda Springs, wood and grass are abundant.
Fort Hall, -	75	1281	The wagon way is very circuitous, but it crosses many creeks and branches, on all of which is an abundance of grass, and on some of them wood. Fort Hall is situated on the bank of Snake river, and in its vicinity, the valley is covered with grass, and the banks of the little streams with trees.
American Falls, -	18	1299	In this distance there are many good places for encampments.
Raft creek, -	23	1322	In this distance there are places suitable for camps, every 4 or 5 miles. Where the trail crosses Raft creek, there is good grass, and plenty of willow brush.
Big Spring, -	16	1338	This is a large marsh, affording very good grass. On the neighboring hills there are cedar trees.
Snake River, -	10	1348	
Goos Creek, -	4	1352	A great abundance of excellent grass, and of willow wood.

	Miles.	Total.	
Snake River, -	23	1375	In this distance the road runs near the river. The water is generally accessible, and in the narrow bottoms there is much good grass.
Dry Fork, -	7	1382	Good grass for a few companies, and willow brush.
Cut Rock Creek. -	12	1394	A large scope of fine grass, and plenty of willow wood.
Cut Rock Creek, -	10	1404	Here the trail crosses the stream, where there is wood and grass sufficient for several large companies. In the last distance, it runs down on the east side of the creek.
Cut Rock Creek, -	12	1416	Here the trail leaves the creek,—some grass and wood.
Snake River, -	15	1431	Impossible to get near it with wagons.
Snake River, -	8	1439	In the intermediate distance it is inaccessible.
Salmon creek, -	5	1444	Good encampment—wood and grass.
Salmon Falls, -	5	1449	Neither wood nor grass.
Crossing, -	27	1476	Here the trail crosses Snake river, which, if it should happen not to be low, will be very difficult to pass. There is not a stick of wood any where near,—good grass In the last distance, there is grass, but no water, without going to the river, which is three or four miles from the trail.
Boise River, -	80	1556	In this distance the country is rough, and there is a scarcity of water and grass. Fine camps on the Boise.
Fort Boise, -	50	1606	In the intermediate distance, the trail follows down the Boise river, along which grass and wood are found, in inexhaustible abundance. Near the fort, grass is scarce. Here the trail recrosses Snake river.
Malheur River, -	12	1618	Good grass, and a little willow brush.
Sulphur Spring, -	11	1629	Some grass, but no wood.
A small branch, -	5	1634	Some grass, and a little willow brush.
Snake River, -	5	1639	do do do.
Brule River. -	3	1642	Good grass and some wood.
Branch of the Brule,	40	1682	In this distance the road which is perhaps the worst on the whole route, follows up the Brule and its branches. There is good grass all along in the narrow bottoms, and there is an abundance of wood.
Fallen Pine, -	24	1706	Water, grass, and some willow brush.
Powder River -	10	1716	Excellent grass in the greatest abundance,—willow brush.
Grand Round, -	15	1731	The Round is covered with superior grass, the streams are fringed with balm and willow trees, and the mountains around are clothed with pines. From this point the trail ascends the main range of the Blue Mountains.
Grand Round River,	16	1747	Good grass, and forests of pine.
A small creek, -	18	1765	But little grass, forests of pine.
Utilla River, -	17	1782	This is a small river at the western base of the Blue Mountains. The bottoms and hills

	Miles.	Total.	
			are covered with a most superior kind of grass, and the banks of the stream, where the trail crosses it, are fringed with various kinds of trees. Here there are two roads, one going by the way of Dr. Whitman's and Fort Walawala, and the other following down the Utilla. The latter is considered to be much the nearest and best.
Mouth of Utilla,	60	1842	In this distance the trail follows the narrow valley of the river which affords generally an abundance of excellent grass. In some places wood is scarce.—Trail leaves it a few miles from the mouth.
Columbia, -	14	1856	Not much grass, and no wood.
A creek, - -	22	1878	Good grass, and some wood. At several places in the last distance, the trail comes near the Columbia.
Columbia, - -	12	1890	Some grass, but no wood.
John Day's River,	20	1910	In this distance the trail runs near the Columbia. At John Days river there is good grass and a little wood.
De Chutes River,	14	1924	Some grass—no wood. Along the Columbia, wood may frequently be purchased from the Indians.
A small creek, -	10	1934	Good grass, and plenty of brush.
Wascopin Mission,	5	1939	The Mission is situated near the Columbia, and in its vicinity, there is an abundance of grass and wood. It is situated at the eastern base of the Cascade Mountains, and here the wagon road terminates. Animals may be driven over the mountains, but wagons and their contents must be taken down the Columbia in boats.
Cascade Falls, -	50	1989	This is the distance by water. The river is smooth and the navigation uninterrupted. At the Falls it is necessary to make a portage of three miles—portage on the North side.—Tide water.
Vancouver, -	40	2029	River smooth unless agitated by wind.
Mouth of Willammette,	6	2035	
Astoria, -	84	2119	
Mouth of Columbia,	12	2131	

NOTE.—Most of the above distances, are according to the daily descisions of our company, returning from Oregon. We believe the proportion to be good, but the sum is too small.